Relationship
GRIT

Relationship
GRIT

A *True Story* with *Lessons*
to *Stay Together, Grow Together,*
and *Thrive Together*

JON
GORDON

KATHRYN
GORDON

WILEY

Published by John Wiley & Sons, Inc., Hoboken, New Jersey.
Published simultaneously in Canada.

For general information on our other products and services or for technical support, please contact our Customer Care Department within the United States at (800) 762-2974, outside the United States at (317) 572-3993 or fax (317) 572-4002.

Wiley publishes in a variety of print and electronic formats and by print-on-demand. Some material included with standard print versions of this book may not be included in e-books or in print-on-demand. If this book refers to media such as a CD or DVD that is not included in the version you purchased, you may download this material at http://booksupport.wiley.com. For more information about Wiley products, visit www.wiley.com.

ISBN 9781119430339 (Hardcover)
ISBN 9781119430742 (ePDF)
ISBN 9781119430735 (ePub)

Printed in the United States of America

SKY10017811_071520

For Jade and Cole. We love you to the moon and back.

Contents

Contents

Introduction

Several years ago, I spoke to Angela Duckworth, who had popularized the term "grit" through her TED talk, book, and research. Grit was at the forefront of discussions I had with my clients in sports, business, and healthcare. Everyone wanted to talk about hiring people with grit, developing grit in their people, and having more grit themselves. But as someone who helps leaders build stronger teams, I kept thinking about team grit. I wondered what makes a team gritty. What are the characteristics of teams that don't give up? As Angela and I discussed her research on grit, I asked her if she had done any research on grit and teams. I told her I had a pretty good idea about what makes team members fight for—instead of against—one another, but I wanted to know if there was research that backed up my ideas and experiences. She said she hadn't done any research on that, but it was a fascinating idea.

I told my wife about my conversation with Angela and she said she didn't need research to know what made a team gritty. My wife said that it's all about relationships and all we had to do was look at our relationship and how we have stayed together through all the ups and downs over the years to understand team grit. A team is made up of people, and the relationships they have with one another will determine what kind of grit they have as a team.

My wife and I then started talking about our relationship and how it was a miracle that we were still together. I was a big jerk early in our marriage and she threatened to leave me if I didn't change. That's a story for later in the book, but let's just say she had every right to leave, and the fact that she didn't still amazes me to this day. The more my wife and I talked, we realized it was more than a miracle that kept us together. We actually did things over the years that saved our marriage and made our marriage stronger. Some of it can only be described as divine intervention and some of it was because of the actions we took to develop grit in our relationship.

We've watched many of our friends get divorced. We've seen so many young couples give up on their marriage when things became difficult early on. We know all the mistakes we made and can't help but see all the mistakes couples make that sabotage their relationship. If we made it and stayed together, so can other couples. The marriage doesn't have to be over. The relationship doesn't have to end. You don't have to give up. You just need some Relationship GRIT to help you stick it out. It won't be easy. If only one person in the relationship wants to make the relationship work, it won't. But if *two people* are committed to making it work and have

Relationship GRIT, you'll not only stay together, you'll learn so much more about yourselves, discover a lot of life lessons along the way, grow as individuals, and become stronger as a team. We want to make it clear that we realize Relationship GRIT isn't for every couple. Some people aren't meant to stay together. But we believe you shouldn't give up without trying everything possible. *Please know if you are dealing with abuse, that's a different story, and we encourage you to seek professional help immediately.*

My wife and I decided to write *Relationship GRIT* to share the lessons we learned to help couples develop stronger relationships and marriages. I'm going to share things from my perspective and you'll hear my wife's perspective, insights, and lessons as well. We thought it would be best for you to hear both of our voices and we hope you enjoy the engaging back-and-forth approach we took. Where we might have disagreed while writing the book, I want you to know that my wife won. After all, the greatest lesson I've learned in 23 years of marriage is that my wife is always right. (I'm kidding, but not really. I share more about that later in the book.)

If you've read some of my books, you might be surprised to learn things about me you didn't know. I felt it was important to be vulnerable, transparent, and real. Yes, it's uncomfortable and a little scary to share our private lives with the public, but we knew we needed to do so to help other couples going through challeng-ing times. A big part of healing is using your pain for a purpose and we hope our past pain and lessons serve a purpose to help you create a deeper, more connected, loving, intimate, and happier relationship. We hope this book helps you realize that you can change and your relationship can change for the better. I wasn't perfect. I had a lot of issues. I made mistakes. But my wife stayed with me. She supported me. She strengthened me. She made me a better man and father. I changed for the bet-ter. I know I wouldn't be who I am without her love and grit over the years.

That's the thing about a relationship. It's two imper-fect people coming together and they have to learn to work out their individual flaws and weaknesses and develop a collective strength. It doesn't happen by acci-dent. It's a process. In this spirit, we want to share our mistakes, lessons, successes, journey, and process with you to help make your relationship stronger. It's a pro-cess we call G-R-I-T. Let's get started with the G.

Relationship
GRIT

Chapter 1

G = God

A cord of three strands is not easily broken.

Magical Moments

(Jon)

Relationships often begin with a fateful meeting, a chance encounter, butterflies in your stomach, or magical moments that cause your union to feel like a fairy tale. Meeting Kathryn was like that for me. I remember seeing her walk toward me. I was 24 years old and had just opened a bar/restaurant in Buckhead, Atlanta. I wasn't looking for a girlfriend. I was just standing outside the front entrance trying to get people to come into my bar so I could grow the business.

When Kathryn approached, I started talking to her. When she stopped, I looked into her eyes and told her she was the most beautiful woman I had ever seen. It wasn't a line. It was true. For me it was love at first sight. For her it took a while. ☺ She responded that I was handsome but then said she couldn't stay. She had to go home. She was on her way to her car after having dinner with a friend. I told her I was having a party Friday night at the bar and said she should come back. She promised she would and said goodbye. When she never showed up Friday night, I was mad at myself for not getting her number and wondered if I would ever see her again.

3

A week later I was attending the Taste of Atlanta charity event with my parents, who were in town visiting. We were walking around sampling dishes from the various food stations when I saw her across the room. I couldn't believe it. I said out loud, "That's her. There she is." I ran over to her as she was talking to some guy and completely interrupted their conversation. I can't even tell you what the guy she was talking to looked like. He was like a blur to me. I was laser-focused on her.

"Hey, do you remember me?" She said yes but was much more interested in eating her Oreo cheesecake than talking to me. "You never came to my party," I said.

"I didn't make it out that night," she said unexcitedly.

"Well, you have to give me your number." I was determined not to leave without it. "I want to take you out," I told her.

She handed me her business card with her number on it. I could tell she did it more so to get rid of me, hoping I would leave her alone, than because she wanted to go out with me. But I had what I needed and was not deterred.

Persistence Pays Off
(Kathryn)

Jon was 24 when I met him. I was 28 and dating successful older men. He seemed so young to me and while I thought he was cute, I wasn't interested in dating a younger man, never mind someone who owned a bar. I grew up in an alcoholic family, and had "partied" pretty hard as a teen into young adulthood. So I stopped everything at the age of 25 and completely changed my life. I was into yoga, clean eating, and juicing. I wasn't interested in bars or bar owners. But I did still love my occasional desserts, so when he came to talk to me at the event he wasn't just someone trying to talk to me. He was someone who was keeping me from my Oreo cheesecake.

I gave him my number to get rid of him but then he called—and called again and again. One night we ended up having a great conversation on the phone about spirituality and God and I realized he was much deeper and more interesting than I had originally thought. I found out he went to Cornell University, an Ivy League graduate who was getting his Master's in teaching at Emory University.

He asked me to go out on a date after our great conversation and I agreed. But that night I didn't feel up to it and canceled on him, so we set another date. I canceled that night as well. I told him I had to wash my hair—an excuse he's never forgotten. We set up another date and yes, I canceled that one too. Then we set up another date and when he called to confirm I told him I didn't feel good and let's reschedule. He said, "Look, you've canceled on me five times now. Either we go out tonight or we are never going out." I was on the other line with a girlfriend and clicked over to tell her what he had said. She started laughing and said, "Ohhh, you should go out with him!" So I clicked over and said okay.

I made no effort to fix my hair or do my makeup. We met at the Tavern at Phipps Plaza and had a nice time talking but it wasn't magical for me. In fact, that upcoming weekend I went on a trip with my friends to Amelia Island in Florida and while walking and talking on the beach with my friends, I decided I needed to simplify my life. I began eliminating the guys I would no longer date. There was a list. Jon wasn't even on the list!

Yet, when I returned home, for reasons I can't explain to this day, he was the first one I called to tell I was back in town. He said, "I'm coming over," and was knocking on my door in no time.

A Divine Appointment
(Jon)

I had no idea she even had a list. I just knew she called me and I wanted to see her again. Our first date was good but it wasn't anything special. But I knew I wanted to spend more time with her. We hung out on her living room couch and talked for hours and hours about God and our paths and the books we read. Looking back, we could have talked about a lot of things, but that was what bonded us.

We weren't religious people. I grew up in a Jewish Italian family and never went to church or temple. Kathryn grew up Irish Catholic but only went to church on Christmas and Easter. Yet we were both very spiritual and read a lot of spiritual books. It was a very special and magical night. I don't even think we kissed once and yet I felt deeply connected to her. After that night I knew without a doubt she was the one for me. It was destiny.

I believed that God brought us together. If I wasn't standing on the corner at the moment she walked by to get to her car, we would never have met. If Kathryn didn't accept an invitation from her friend to go to the Taste of Atlanta event the following week, we might never have seen each other again.

A Deeper Connection
(Kathryn)

We were inseparable after that. Our spiritual conversations bonded us together and gave me a window into Jon's soul. He was a deep thinker with an old soul. We both had dated a lot.

Our past relationships were more surface level and based on physical attraction, but this was different. This went beyond the physical. In fact, the physical didn't go well in the beginning. The kissing was awkward. The

G = God

first time we had sex was a disaster. (Yes, you read that right—I'm going there.) Yet, we liked each other and had a soul connection that bonded us together.

I used to walk/run this same route in a suburban Atlanta neighborhood behind my apartment complex. I would stop at what came to be known as my "God tree." And I would pray my prayers before heading back up to my apartment. I started taking Jon on walks to my God tree. It became our "thing."

So it was especially meaningful when he proposed to me under "our" God tree six months later. We were connected at a deeper level and that was a good thing, because we would need a greater connection to weather the storms ahead.

A Triple-Braided Cord
(Jon)

There would be many storms ahead in our relationship, as you are about to learn. But the fact that our bond was based on our talks about God—our spiritual conversations and soul connection—is one of the big reasons why I believe we stayed together when we could easily have given up.

Looking back and observing how this kept us together is why we believe the G in "Grit" stands for God and why God is so important not just for our relationship but any relationship.

Please know when we are talking about God we are not talking about religion. When we met we were both what would be considered spiritual new-agers who loved Deepak Chopra, Wayne Dyer, and Gary Zukov. We were more Buddhist than Christian or Jewish, and we went to spiritual seminars, not church. But if you know about addiction programs, you know they all include a higher power. That's because you can't beat the addiction on your own. You are not strong enough. You need a higher power to give you strength when you are weak. You need a greater source of power to keep going when you want to give up.

It's the same way in a relationship or marriage. When you make God the center of your relationship you are not just going through life as two cords but three cords. Two cords bound together are good. But with a third cord, the bond is much stronger. God is the third cord you need in your relationship. We know because while God brought us together, after we got engaged God seemed to leave us alone or we seemed to leave God alone. And our relationship as two cords went downhill very quickly.

Chapter 2

R = Resolve

It's often easier to give up and walk away.
Relationships require a desire to stay together
and a willingness to change for the better.

From Fantasy to Reality
(Kathryn)

Jon and I were engaged six months after meeting. It seemed that once he put the ring on my finger, we started fighting a lot. This is when it got real. All of our issues and insecurities reared their ugly heads. Jon was so jealous. I couldn't even talk to another guy without him getting mad. I was scared of committing and tried to break up with him several times. Jon would say, "You are just scared," and it made me feel better because I knew he was right.

I suggested we get some counseling. Jon was reluctant (as I find most men are), but he finally agreed to go. We saw a female therapist and at the first meeting we began to talk about some of the issues we were fighting about. She actually laughed out loud at us. For the life of me I can't remember exactly what I said but I know it wasn't funny! Jon and I just looked at each other. In a strange way it bonded us. We had a common enemy. The therapist who laughed at us would never see us again!

Unfortunately, this made Jon even more reluctant to go to another therapist. So I thought seeing a male counselor might make Jon feel more at ease. I found

"Sean," a nice man with an easy presence. Five minutes into asking us some probing questions, Jon and I started fighting. Okay, maybe I started fighting. The therapist said to me, "Wow, you go from zero to 60 just like that!" and he snapped his fingers. Jon was smirking. I was livid. But I couldn't lose my cool because I knew Jon needed to feel like he had some leverage. We saw "Sean" for several months and he did help us iron out some things, but honestly, I think what bonded us the most was laughing at what he said to me.

To this day, anytime I get mad—and yes, I can be quick tempered; I'm Irish after all—Jon will snap his fingers and say, "Wow you go from zero to 60 just like that," and we will start laughing.

Well, most of the time.

Issues of the Past
(Jon)

Looking back, everything happened so fast. It was a whirlwind. Kathryn and I had just met and the next thing I know we are living together and engaged. I was in love but not mature enough to have a healthy relationship.

That's the thing about relationships. It brings together two people who carry with them their imperfections, flaws, issues, and wounds, and somehow, some way, you have to find a way to make it work.

Kathryn was very friendly with people, including men, and I was very jealous. I was 24 and I was crazy about her. I didn't want to lose her. My biological father left when I was a year old and it left me with some deep wounds and abandonment issues. He stayed in our life and we saw him some weekends and on some holidays, but he remarried and had a new family and my brother and I always felt like second fiddle.

I would find out later in life that he didn't want my mom to have me. They were not in a good place in their relationship and the last thing he wanted was another child—and that child was me.

My mom remarried when I was five and Joe became my dad. He was a New York City police officer who saw the world as a dangerous place and taught us to be tough and strong to take it on. He was honestly one of the most negative guys on the planet but very loving to his family. He was a great father who took me and my brother on as his own and raised us with love. But for some reason I often had this feeling that I wasn't good enough.

On the outside I was a hard worker who achieved some success at a young age. But in my relationships, I wasn't secure enough in myself. I didn't really know who I was at this point in my life. So here I am getting married to someone I don't really know well while not really knowing myself at the same time. Going to counseling helped a lot and having Sean validate me and

R = Resolve

Kathryn's quick temper felt good. But it didn't stop me from being jealous and causing us to fight. I was still insecure and would point out her flaws to make myself feel better while making Kathryn feel worse.

Even though she had a quick temper, she was very sweet, loving, and caring and unfortunately received my worst rather than my best. I would let my jealousy, fear, and stress about our wedding and future get the best of me and say something mean, which would begin another fight. Going to counseling and acknowledging our problems early on was key because we brought them to light instead of covering them up and allowing them to fester. This wouldn't heal my issues or provide a permanent solution, but it helped at the time.

It Takes Two
(Kathryn)

Jon had his issues and I definitely had mine. I grew up in a home with both Mom, Dad, and two older brothers. We were a Navy family so I moved around quite a bit early in my childhood. I went to five different elementary schools between Maine and Florida before settling in Virginia Beach, Virginia, at nine years old. My mother was an amazing cook and the house was always spotless. My father was a naval flight engineer. Dad and I had a wonderful relationship. He played the guitar and I sang from as early as three years old. So my home seemed "normal" from the outside. But it wasn't.

There were many alcohol-fueled nights of my parents having horrible fights, screaming and yelling that many times escalated into physical violence. Some of these fights were brought on when one of my dad's many trysts would call the house to tell my mom of my dad's infidelities.

So, I definitely came into our relationship with trust and commitment issues. I had a hard time trusting men and because I was scared of getting hurt, I tried to break up with Jon several times. Not to mention the fact that I liked attention and was friendly (Jon would say flirty), which fueled his insecurities. And when he would say hurtful things, I didn't just take it. I would fight back. So we had a lot of shouting matches.

Despite my issues with commitment, I did do one thing that was very helpful for our relationship. Before we met, Jon had started a nonprofit called the Phoenix Organization. It was a group of young professionals who supported youth-focused charities. He was always going to an event or organizing his own gala to raise money for organizations such as the Boys and Girls Club. I was very immersed in the social culture of Atlanta as well. There were power struggles when he thought something he was doing was important, but I thought what I was doing was important. I found myself starting to compete with him.

This was a very pivotal time for us. I realized I had to make a decision for this relationship to work. At that time we both couldn't be out there, so I had to resolve to get behind him. Now I am *not* saying that that is what a woman has to do. I'm not saying that's what a man has to do. There are many successful couples who can do both. But in our situation at that time, that's what I needed to do to make our relationship work. And so I did.

This was a very big decision for me because of my upbringing. I swore that I would never take a back seat to a man. It was definitely a leap of faith, but I believe that if I went the other way, our relationship wouldn't have survived.

Buying a House
(Jon)

If getting married wasn't stressful enough, three months after our engagement we decided to buy a house. My bar/restaurant had started to do very well and after the Olympics we had enough money to make a down payment on a house. Neither of us had made a purchase like this before but we decided to go for it. Even though we were fighting a lot, we were still planning on getting married and starting a family. I'm not sure why I felt we needed a house right away, but we found one pretty quickly and went through the mortgage process for the first time.

When I met Kathryn, I was renting a room in my friend's house. Now, less than a year later, I was buying a house where my future wife and children would live. Talk about stressful. Every decision I made seemed to create more stress, but I just kept plowing ahead.

Ain't No Stopping Us
(Kathryn)

To add to our relationship challenges, three months before our wedding my mother died of cancer. We were married on May 17, 1997. My mother was diagnosed with cancer in October 1996 and passed away four short months later on February 19, 1997. I was flying back and forth to Virginia to be with her during that time. I was with her when she passed that day and I'll always be grateful I was there.

When I returned home it was full speed ahead toward the wedding. The truth is, I never really grieved properly because I was so focused on getting married and making the event special. Jon was supportive but wasn't emotionally mature enough to talk about it or ask me how I was doing.

Ironically, we were getting married but we were growing further apart. We fought more than ever and really didn't like each other at the time. Yet there was still a feeling of deep love and commitment so we just kept moving forward with our marriage plans. It sounds weird now to type this, but that's how it happened.

Big Decisions

(Jon)

It's hard to explain. I didn't like Kathryn at the time but I knew I loved her. I knew I couldn't walk away even though there were times I wanted to. And I know there were times when Kathryn wanted to leave me. Our issues were taking their toll. But I think it was the meaningful conversations we had in the beginning, a knowledge that we were supposed to be together, and occasional moments of love and laughter that kept us going. When I would stand in the kitchen and look at her, I knew she was the one for me. I couldn't imagine anyone else being my wife. So we pressed on.

The wedding was beautiful and the day was amazing. Our families and friends were there at the Japanese gardens of the Hotel Nikko, now the Grand Hyatt Hotel in Buckhead. It was a day I made the biggest decision of my life, but at the time I didn't appreciate the commitment I was making, the vows I recited, or the fact that I was taking on this woman to be my wife. I was young and clueless and focused more on my future goals and success than our marriage.

Right after we returned from our honeymoon, I decided to run for the city council of Atlanta. I was an economics and government major in college and always wanted to go into politics. For some reason I decided this was a good time. Nothing like starting off your new marriage by running for political office and asking your new wife to help run your campaign.

Kathryn addressed and sent out hundreds and hundreds of postcards and made phone calls while I walked to every house in the district—7000 houses! It was grueling and eye opening. I took the lead in the polls and the other candidates made up lies about me and attacked me. I was only 26, yet they found things to make up.

It was a very close election but I lost. I thought my life was over. Even though I had a successful restaurant business, my real hopes and dreams were squashed. I've learned that sometimes you have to lose a goal to find your destiny. Yet at the time it was painful and only revved up my thinking about what I could do next to further myself and be successful. I believed I had to be successful to prove to others that I was worthy. I needed to fill my ego with accomplishments.

So even though I was married, I was really focused on myself and my own success. This wasn't a good thing because we were about to have a baby.

We're Having a Baby

(Kathryn)

Honestly, besides the fact that I loved him, one of the reasons I stayed with Jon and married him was because

I wanted children. I had told my friends that if it didn't work out, at least I'd have my children.

During his city council run I got pregnant. I didn't think I could because of several issues I had when I was younger, so when I found out, I was very surprised, but not as surprised as Jon. When I told Jon, he said, "But I'm not ready." I replied, "You better get ready because you don't have a choice. The baby is coming."

During Lamaze class he was laughing and was not engaged. I told him I didn't think he was serious about this. He said, "Don't worry. I'm good on game day." Good on game day? What the hell does that mean? Who says that?

I chose to have a natural childbirth, which sounded great in theory but took 15 hours with no pain meds. It was primal and exhausting. But I have to give Jon credit. He *was* good on game day. He kept encouraging me to breathe, at which point I lovingly told him to shut the f*ck up. But then our beautiful baby Jade was born with her eyes wide open. I held her and Jon held her and life was perfect—for the moment.

A Living Hell
(Kathryn)

I grew up in Virginia Beach in the '80s. It was a crazy time. I was doing a lot of modeling back then. One of the assignments I was often called for were bikini ads for the local magazines and tourist books.

Several of my friends had gotten breast implants. I decided I was going to do it as well. I walked into my local bank and told the bank manager I wanted to take out a loan to get breast implants. I think he was taken aback that I had the nerve to actually go in and ask. He gave me a loan for $2500 and I got my breast implants in June 1988. In all honesty, I did not need breast implants. I was perfectly fine the way I was. But everyone was doing it!

Fast forward to birthing my daughter. I was able to breastfeed, which I had wanted to do. Thank God! Or so I thought. . . .

Jade was not able to latch on. She was tongue tied, so she couldn't feed properly. We had her tongue clipped and continued with the breastfeeding. Around the end of week three she developed thrush in her mouth. And I got mastitis, which is an infection of a clogged milk duct. I didn't even know what was happening. I was lying in my room with a fever. A friend came in and looked at me, then looked at my chest and said, "Kathryn, you have mastitis. You need to get to the doctor." Thank God for her. Mastitis is common but I probably would have gotten very ill before I knew what was happening. She stayed with Jade and I went to the doctor. I indeed had a bad case of mastitis.

As my mastitis was healing, I then started feeling fatigued and my body ached. My joints were hot and painful. Although there were several issues at this point, one situation stands out. I was in the kitchen doing dishes. I wasn't getting any sleep. I had a newborn baby. I was feeling so achy. I was trying to adjust to everything and I just started crying. Jon was not supportive during this time at all and he said to me, "You're going to have to get it together. I can't help you," and walked out of the house. (Jon says he's been paying for this ever since!)

Throughout the next nine months, I would continue to get sicker and sicker. I had hot and tender joints, I would get numbness and tingling up my neck and down my legs. I was starting to occasionally slur my words. My feet would feel like they were on fire. I was foggy. My chest would itch from the inside out so I would beat on it to try to scratch it even though that hurt.

I went to my ob-gyn and she said I had postpartum depression. I didn't feel depressed! I felt sick, like I had the flu. I went to a rheumatologist. He said it probably had something to do with having just had a baby. Then I started having nerve pain and numbness so I went to a neurologist, who did a series of nerve tests, sticking little needles in my calves. Nothing remarkable.

Back then they were prescribing OxyContin like it was Tylenol. So I had four bottles full. But in my gut I knew there was truly something wrong with me. So I didn't want to medicate myself. I had to find out what was really going on. But I held on to the medication "just in case."

I would beg Jon to come home from law school (he decided to go after his failed city council bid) to watch Jade so I could go to yet another doctor. He was always so stressed and angry. My baby would cry and I would shudder.

Every time I would come home from the doctor without a diagnosis it would exacerbate Jon's frustration. The doctors said nothing was wrong with me and *everyone,* including Jon, thought I was crazy. By this point I was worn down, exhausted, and hopeless. I was starting to have a hard time with normal functioning. My head hung down. I was losing my will to fight for myself. I was getting no answers and no help. So I made a decision.

I went to bed that night and I prayed to God that I would be forgiven for what I was going to do. I prayed that my mother-in-law and Jon would take care of my baby Jade. My plan was that when Jon went to law school the next morning, I would take all the pills and end this nightmare.

But that night I had a dream. And I heard a very crisp loud voice say, "Your breast implants are making you sick." I woke up that morning and rolled over and told Jon about my dream. And for the first time in months he looked at me with a gleam in his eyes and said, "I believe you. I'll take a second mortgage out on the house to get my wife back. Whatever it takes!"

R = Resolve

I would love to say this is when he became an amazing, supportive, loving husband, but it wasn't. He wouldn't even drive me to get the surgery to remove my implants. A friend drove me, and also drove me home after the surgery. She came by for several days to check on me.

It turned out that the breast implants were filled with a fungus called *Aspergillus nigus,* or black mold. Little did I know that systemic fungal *and* bacterial infections were attacking my body! So I wasn't crazy! If you want to know more about that story, google Kathryn Gordon breast implants and you can read about it.

About three weeks after the implant removal surgery, I woke up one morning and I couldn't stand up. Every time I would try to stand, I would fall down. I asked Jon to help me but he told me he couldn't and left for class. My neighbor across the street drove me to the ER and dropped me off. That was a horrible experience. I had no one looking out for me.

They diagnosed me with an inner ear infection and gave me something in the ER to treat it. Next thing I knew I had severe chills and was shaking uncontrollably. I kept calling out for someone to help me. Finally someone came over and said it looked like I was reacting to the medicine. So they gave me something else. I finally stopped getting the chills and shakes and was able to stand enough to walk over to use the phone. I called my husband and asked him to pick me up and he said he couldn't come get me. So I called my neighbor, who picked me up and brought me home.

Busy, Stressed, and Selfish
(Jon)

After losing the city council election, I decided to go to law school. My mom had always wanted me to be a lawyer and I had planned to go after college. When I didn't get into the law schools I wanted to go to, I put it on hold. But now I felt I had unfinished business and needed to go. We had several bar/restaurants at this time that were basically running themselves, so I decided to apply. I was accepted, with the help of a recommendation from a Supreme Court Justice of Georgia, Leah Sears.

I had been featured in a bunch of magazines as one of Atlanta's rising stars. I owned popular bars/restaurants, ran a nonprofit that was making a difference in the community, was politically connected after my city council run, and yet I was a horrible husband. I admit it. I was terrible. I was achieving success but failing miserably at home. Everyone thought I was great except my wife.

Law school caused me a lot of stress and because I was so busy with class and studying and handling the marketing for the restaurants and all my nonprofit initiatives, I didn't make time to help Kathryn when she needed me most. She was an inconvenience to me, choosing the worst possible time to get sick. Didn't she know I had a lot on my plate? It was so selfish of me but that's how I saw it at the time.

I remember just starting law school and feeling the pressure of the first week of classes. Kathryn was crying, dealing with what I thought was postpartum depression. All the doctors said she was fine, so I thought it was all in her head. Here we were newly married with a baby. I was 27 years old, and when she got sick, I didn't know how to handle it. I wasn't mature enough or compassionate enough at the time. She said to me, "I really need your help." I said, "I can't help you right now. I have a lot on my plate. You need to suck it up and deal with it."

Why I Stayed
(Kathryn)

You may be wondering why I didn't leave Jon after all this. As I said earlier, I grew up in an alcoholic family. I saw good people do bad things. I saw a family that fought a lot but they carried on the next day. They didn't get divorced. They stayed together. I'm not saying it's a good thing, but it's what I saw and what I knew. I think I also stayed because I was fighting for my life. I was just trying to get better.

I had seen the goodness in him early on. I kept asking where that guy was who would notice I was out of perfume and go to the store and buy me some. I had seen such sweetness at the beginning of our relationship. My upbringing taught me to take the bad in my life and see how it can be used for good. Transferring to five different elementary schools in the middle of the school year taught me how to make friends and dive into social situations. It also taught me how to wing it! I had no choice. It might have been horrible the night before in my home, but you woke up and you went to work or school and you carried on.

I think this trait helped me in my sales career later on. I could take rejection and let things roll off my back and go for the next sale. I think this also allowed me to weather my relationship with Jon early on.

Let me be clear, there was no physical or psychological abuse. If you are in an abusive relationship, you should seek professional help immediately.

I did a lot of therapy around my childhood and upbringing. (This is the abbreviated version because I don't want this book to be about my alcoholic, dysfunctional home.) I'm sharing here to show how I chose to see my life circumstances and how it affected my thoughts and actions in my relationship with Jon at the time. Growing up in an alcoholic home, I saw great people acting badly. So I learned to compartmentalize as one of my coping mechanisms.

I progressively got better and really worked on trying to heal my body. Two months after I had my implants removed, I got pregnant with our son Cole. So that became my focus.

After I had Cole I was being contacted by lots of media outlets to tell my breast implant story. *Glamour* magazine did a story on me. I shot several documentaries. I flew up to New York City and did *The Montel Williams Show*. I had made a deal with God that if he healed me and made it possible to take care of my babies that I would share my implant story to help other women.

Chasing Success
(Jon)

After a year and a half of law school, I quit. I walked out of my exams without taking the tests and never looked back. I had an opportunity to work in business development for a start-up dot.com that connected data from mainframe computers to mobile devices. It was at the forefront of the mobile revolution and I saw it as a huge opportunity to make my millions. By this time I knew I didn't want to be a lawyer and this was an exciting new venture that would allow me to create the success I craved.

There was one challenge, however. I had never worked in an office before and this job required me to work at an office each day. The first few months were exciting and new but soon after that I began to feel like

I was in a cage, trapped in my pursuit of money and success. I had always been my own boss and now I had a boss. I had always been entrepreneurial running my own business, campaign, and nonprofit and now I had to create sales pipelines and demonstrate progress. I had sacrificed happiness for 80,000 shares and the potential of becoming dot.com rich. To make matters worse, we weren't generating any sales or revenue.

I did secure a deal with the NFL and we were the first to bring NFL scores to mobile devices. It was a big win for the company and me, but we did it on a non-revenue pilot basis to show our technology. People loved to see what we could do but no one wanted to pay for it. Like most dot.com companies at the time, no one cared about making money. We were spending a lot and making almost nothing.

During this period I was devoting less and less time to the bar/restaurants and my dividend checks as an owner became smaller and smaller. When I questioned my partners about why I wasn't receiving as much money, they blew me off. When I asked to see the books, they offered to buy me out. I really didn't have a choice, so I agreed. They offered me a quarter of what I thought I deserved but I didn't want to get into a legal battle and accepted their offer.

I was officially out of the restaurant business. I was no longer an entrepreneur. I now worked for dot .com entrepreneurs. A friend of mine was running the nonprofit I started. So the only thing left for me was working for a dot.com where I was miserable, and I was being a miserable husband and a miserable father to my two young children.

Making the Move
(Jon)

Around this time Kathryn and I started talking about moving. She grew up in Virginia Beach and I grew up on Long Island so we both wanted to move to the beach. We made a list: Tampa, San Diego, and someone said to check out Jacksonville. After seeing an advertisement in a magazine about a community in Ponte Vedra Beach near Jacksonville, Kathryn and I decided to take a drive with the kids to check it out.

After visiting a number of homes we couldn't afford, we were heading home when we saw a restaurant that looked good and decided to eat there. As we approached the restaurant, we saw a real estate office next door and walked in to see if they had any places for rent. When we told the woman we couldn't afford anything in town, she asked us our price range and said she had a few places in mind for us to see.

The first place she showed us we decided to buy. I truly believe it was fate. If we had driven away without stopping at the restaurant, we would never have come back to Jacksonville. We wrote up a contract, went back to Atlanta, and put our home on the market. My plan was to work in Atlanta during the week and drive to Ponte Vedra for the weekends. But when I told my boss about buying a new home and my plans to go home on the weekends, he said that wouldn't be good for my marriage and that I could work from my home office in Florida.

Within a few months of the move, the dot.com I was working for was running out of cash and sinking faster than the *Titanic*. I had a new home, a wife, and two small children, and felt more stress and pressure than ever. If I lost my job, what would I do? How would I provide for my family?

I prayed and asked what I was born to do. Writing and speaking came to me. I didn't know what I would write and speak about, but I knew I wanted to inspire others the way I was inspired by the books I read.

But I couldn't just do this right away and support my family. I needed to find a way to make money while I started writing. I was good at the restaurant business, so I decided to combine the money from taking a second mortgage on our home and from selling my restaurants in Atlanta with a $20,000 loan on my credit card to open a Moe's Southwest Grill in Jacksonville. We were the first Moe's in Florida and only the sixth Moe's in existence. My goal was to open the restaurant and have a manager run it while I still worked for the dot.com.

R = Resolve

However, two weeks before we opened, I got the call from my boss. He said I had survived longer than most but I was now fired. My face turned pale. Only two weeks' severance. No insurance for my family. All my money tied up in a restaurant that was about to open and would take a while to turn a profit or would possibly fail. I went downstairs and told Kathryn the bad news. She said, "It's going to be okay. We will find a way."

I went back upstairs and just broke down and cried. I prayed to God, "Please provide for me and my family and I will do your work. I will make a difference in this world." I'll never forget the feeling of peace that came over me. I was filled with the belief that this had all happened for a reason.

Whatever It Takes
(Kathryn)

It's amazing what you'll do when your family's future is on the line. Jon and I put Moe's "now open" fliers on cars parked at the movie theater near our new restaurant and brought catering menus to local businesses. When I wasn't taking care of the kids, I was helping him market and also getting my résumé ready to go back to work. If things didn't turn around soon, I was going to apply at Starbucks, knowing they provided insurance.

In the beginning, Jon worked at the restaurant all the time and I did the accounting and handled all the bills. We were a team but he was still not easy to be around. He fluctuated between positive moods with great hope and expectations and angry outbursts. He always took his frustration and stress out on me. We were so close to going bankrupt and fought about money all the time. Not to mention I was still sick and dealing with undiagnosed celiac disease. I still had a lot of fatigue and achy joints and once again doctors didn't know what was wrong with me.

Miracles
(Jon)

I was stressed a lot because I knew if this restaurant went under, we would be bankrupt and homeless. Everything we owned was tied up in Moe's. We had no savings and no backup plan if the restaurant didn't make money. For the first time I wasn't in control. For the first time I was brought to my knees and I surrendered to God. It was as if everything was stripped away from me and I was forced to rely on God.

This is where my faith was truly born. I prayed every day for a miracle, and the miracles came. We broke even the first week at the restaurant. That was a miracle. We broke even the second week. An old friend who owed me money suddenly called me and paid me back and we were able to pay our home mortgage. We broke even the third week. We were getting tired of eating at Moe's but we had no choice. I sold a Moe's franchise to someone and received a commission for that, and that paid our mortgage the next month.

Then out of the blue an acquaintance I didn't even know that well called me to ask if I would meet with a company in Jacksonville that wanted to learn about wireless technology. I told them I didn't know how the technology worked. They said we don't need you to tell us how it works; we just want to know how to sell it. They offered me $13,000 for six weeks of consulting to teach them how to sell it.

I couldn't believe it. It was a miraculous gift that came out of nowhere. That money carried us for a few months as we continued to market Moe's and began advertising on the radio. The radio ads worked well and business grew. And as we used up the last of the $13,000 consulting money to pay our bills, our Moe's made its first profit and business boomed after that.

I wish I could say I became Mr. Positive after we started making some money, but I didn't. Kathryn was right about my outbursts. I was often stressed and negative. I would pray and feel good for a while but the minute I would get hit with challenges from the restaurant I would become a jerk. I still let the pressure and stress of running a restaurant and providing for my family get the best of me. While I had become a praying person, I wasn't a positive person.

I Was Ready to Leave Him
(Kathryn)

Unfortunately, here I was again not feeling well. I thought it was all behind me with the breast implant debacle in Atlanta. But I was extremely achy and lethargic. And I now I had two very rowdy little children to take care of and an absent husband. I plowed through my days and prayed for relief. But Jon would come home and make matters worse.

On one particular day I had about 20 things that had to be done for the restaurant while dealing with the kids. I managed to get everything done except one thing that I would need to do the next day. I ran to the grocery store, shopped, and got home to make dinner. Jon walked in the door and asked me about the *one* thing I didn't get done.

I just lost it. It was the last straw. We yelled and screamed at each other and I made a decision right then. I am leaving him. I told him I would do whatever it took to get away from him and support myself and my children. He stormed out of the house.

He kept calling and I finally answered. We tried to talk but started fighting again. I told him he was just so miserable all the time. He said, "It's because of you. You make me miserable." My heart sank. I had no fight left. I started crying. I said, "Oh wow. Okay. Then we definitely shouldn't stay together." I hung up. That really hit me hard. And I certainly didn't want to be with someone if I made them miserable.

The next thing I knew, Jon was there, telling me he was so sorry. He started crying and begged me to stay. He promised he would change.

I knew he also suffered from depression. I told him he had to get help. He said he wanted to try to deal with it on his own first. I was skeptical, but he was able to manage his moods by food, exercise, and meditation and prayer.

The Ultimatum
(Jon)

Kathryn gave me an ultimatum and I'm glad she did. I needed it. It woke me up. I looked in the mirror at 31 years old and didn't like who I had become. I needed to change. I always blamed her for why I wasn't happy. It was everyone else's fault but my own. Kathryn's ultimatum caused me to own my attitude and actions.

In the early years I resented my wife and kids. I felt they were in my way and the reason why I wasn't as successful as I wanted to be. After Jade was born, instead of focusing more on my marriage and family, I looked for opportunities to escape.

I made the mistake some young fathers make during the early years of marriage and looked outside my marriage for attention. I had several too-close encounters with women that violated the trust Kathryn had in me. While these were not sexual affairs or emotional entanglements, they were momentary flings where I was being distracted by women outside my marriage. I'm not proud of this. But I'm also not afraid to tell the truth.

At the time, however, I was afraid to tell Kathryn, and didn't tell her until years later. When I did tell her, she went from zero to 60 faster than I've ever seen. We'll share more about that later in the book. It's part of our story and made us who we are together.

A Defining Moment
(Jon)

Kathryn's ultimatum was one of the most defining moments in my life. It was after that when I realized that one of the reasons I was miserable was because I wasn't doing what I was born to do. I was angry because I had so much to share with the world but it was trapped inside my negative shell. I was meant to write and speak and now I had to go for it. I had to live and share my purpose.

I wanted to be more positive, so I began to research ways I could be more positive. I read that you can't be

39

R = Resolve

stressed and thankful at the same time, so I started taking thank-you walks each day where I would walk and say what I was thankful for and then pray. I launched a weekly newsletter where I would share a new positive tip.

I met people at Moe's who would invite me to speak to their company. My first talk was "Success Is All about the Little Things." I gave free talks to any group who would let me speak. Over time, I came to believe that I could actually do this for a career.

Most of all I worked to be a better person, husband, and father. I was far from perfect, but I improved.

You Have to Be Willing to Change
(Jon)

I hear from a lot of people who get divorced that their spouse gave them an ultimatum but they were too prideful to change. The way I see it, you will have to change at some point. If not during your first marriage, you'll have to change if you want to stay married during your second one. You'll repeat the same pattern and mistakes if you don't look in the mirror and address the problem. If *you* don't change, nothing will.

When you change, you are able to change your relationship for the better. Deciding to change was the best thing that ever happened to me and subsequently to my wife and kids. I learned that changing for the better doesn't take a lot of talent or skill. It just takes a willingness and desire to be better for yourself and the people around you. You have to be willing to look at your flaws and ask how you can improve. You have to be willing to be uncomfortable as you remove old bad habits and replace them with good habits. You have to be willing to make others a priority. You have to be willing to invest in yourself and your relationship and family.

This leads us to the next section where the "I" in G-R-I-T stands for Invest.

Chapter 3

I = Invest

To have a great relationship you can't act like you are two separate teams. You must invest time and energy to become one team who supports and encourages each other.

Invest Instead of Consume
(Jon)

In a marriage you can be a consumer or an investor. You can give or take from the marriage. I was a consumer in my marriage early on, taking what I needed for me and being upset when Kathryn needed me to give my time and energy.

But then I became more focused on being an investor. I was no longer looking outside my marriage. I was investing in it. And once I started investing in my marriage, everything improved.

I was still very busy with my restaurants. The first Moe's did really well, so we opened a few more since finding financial investors was easy. I was also speaking a lot, giving free talks around town to anyone who would have me speak. And I made time to write each week and continued to work on myself and feed myself with positivity each day.

But even with all that, I made time to become more involved as a husband and father. I was no longer an absent member of the family. Rather than considering my wife and kids a burden and liability, I realized they were an investment I needed to make. It wasn't a huge investment at this time; that would come later.

I was still very focused and driven to make my restaurants a success and become a writer and speaker, but my mind-set and perspective had shifted from consuming to investing. I was more self-aware of the instances when I was being narcissistic and negative and was able to stop myself from going down the negative spiral.

In no way was I perfect. I still had a lot of issues to work through. I still had angry outbursts at times. Whenever something happened to one of the kids, I blamed Kathryn for it. At the time I felt like she wasn't focused on their safety enough. Looking back, I know she was a great mother. I was just unreasonably neurotic.

One time Cole had a febrile seizure from a high fever and Kathryn called me in a panic when she thought he had died. She didn't know at the time it was just a seizure. I raced home from the restaurant and as the ambulance was taking him to the hospital I yelled at her as if it was her fault. I was a recovering jerk who had relapses. I was very stressed when my kids were playing in the street. They had a lot of energy and I was very nervous when we would go places. I was worried they would get hurt. Traveling with them was a nightmare for me.

It wasn't like I became a great man all of a sudden. I was a work in progress. I had a long way to go, but I was heading in the right direction. I did want to be better. Life and stress would just get the best of me at times.

Kathryn, on the other hand, was the ultimate investor. She was the one who was making the bigger investment in our marriage and family at the time. Yes, I was working to create a good life for us—one that didn't involve losing our home—but she was giving everything she had to me and the children. She was our rock. My energy was frenetic. Her energy was stable.

I didn't appreciate her selflessness at the time. We were both so busy and trying to make it all work. But now I see so clearly how much she gave, how much she supported me and the kids, and how hard she worked to be a great mother and wife. She deserved better.

Don't Keep Score
(Kathryn)

It's important to understand that it's not going to be equal all the time. There will be times you give more and there will be times your mate gives more. But there is a season for everything. For example, if your wife is having a baby, you're going to give more at that time. If one of you travels for work, the other one is going to have to give more at home.

Early on with our kids I was doing everything. Taking the kids to school, playdates, sports practices, doctors, doing homework and projects, paying the bills for the restaurants, making sales calls to get Jon speaking engagements, and more. I wasn't joyful about it all the time. I didn't always do it all willingly with a smile on my face. Sometimes, I would get exhausted and bitter. On those days, as soon as Jon would walk in the door I would say "I'm *out!*" And I would hop in my car and go to the mall, get a coffee, and just wander from shop to shop. I needed a break.

Jon certainly wasn't always happy about it. Understandably, he was exhausted himself coming home from running the restaurants, but he still did it. In the past he didn't help at all, no matter how tired I was, so we were making progress. But it wasn't a romantic time for us. It was hard, stressful, and felt like we were battling to survive.

And that's the thing about investing. It's not always easy or convenient. One might give more one week, month, or year than the other. Whatever you do, do not keep score. If you keep score in a relationship, you both will lose. It's a team effort and you have to make sure you are communicating during these challenging times. Which leads me to the next important piece—communication.

Communicate, Communicate, Communicate
(Kathryn)

Where there is a void, negativity will fill it.

This is my favorite quote by Jon. I honestly think he has become such a great teacher of communication because early on he was so bad at it. He didn't communicate very well and we had a lot of voids. But it was something I continued to press on.

I always tried to get him to talk things out. I wouldn't accept "nothing" as an answer when I asked what was wrong. I didn't leave him alone when he didn't want to talk about it. (Well, I might leave him alone temporarily but I would always address it later.) I wouldn't let the day end without sharing how I felt about something I was upset about. I can count on one hand the number of times we went to bed angry. Jon slept on the couch those nights, and even then we would get up and talk about what was bothering us.

We didn't always agree, but communication was essential. It was not easy. Yet doing it led to a deeper understanding of each other. Sometimes you have to be uncomfortable and talk about hard stuff. If neither one of you is a skilled communicator, it might be good to have a therapist help in this area.

In Jon's book, *The Power of a Positive Team,* he talks about the importance of having difficult conversations to become a stronger team. It works the same way in a relationship. You have to talk about your issues and challenges if you want to improve and grow together. Ignoring the problems doesn't make them go away; they fester inside and eventually lead to bigger issues, challenges, bad behavior, and too often separation. We know couples who never fought or talked about the hard stuff. I think we surprised a lot of people and ourselves that we are still together because we fought so much. And several of the couples who didn't are divorced. I believe it's because we addressed our issues and always brought them to light.

When you shine a light on the problem, the darkness dissolves, leading to a healthier relationship.

The Curse of Expectations
(Kathryn)

One of the big reasons communication is so essential is because when you are in a relationship you have expectations of how the other person should think and act. If you are always feeling like your spouse doesn't meet your expectations or you can't live up to the expectations they have of you, your relationship will be a disaster.

Our biggest fights had to do with the curse of expectations. Jon was a type A personality who wanted the house clean all the time and I was ADD—fine with getting to it when the urge hit me and with having piles of paperwork that visually reminded me of what I needed to do and who I needed to call. Jon washed his dishes as soon as he was done eating and I was okay leaving mine in the sink. (He still washes the dishes right away and I sometimes still leave mine in the sink.) Jon was a planner and I was spontaneous. Jon was worried about the future. I lived for today. Jon was happiest alone writing in solitude. I was happiest in a room full of friends. In Jon's eyes I didn't cook enough, clean enough, or focus enough on things that mattered to him. But I was doing the best I could.

He would come home and ask me what I did all day. (That would make me go from zero to 60!) In the craziness of the day I couldn't even remember all I did. But it was a lot. I felt like I could never live up to Jon's expectations. Don't get me wrong; I admired Jon's military-type scheduled regimen. He got up at the same time. Did the same walk and workout and stuck to the same daily schedule.

I wanted to be more structured like him. But I would never be like him and I would sometimes tell him that maybe he needed someone more military like he was. I was just wired differently. I was more easygoing. Laid back. Not so intense. But then he would apologize, we would talk about it, and both try to be better for each other until we would fight again a few months later about the same things. Then we would communicate and fight some more.

It was a cycle that went on for a long time, but we did communicate our expectations to each other and stuck it out and learned to work together. Over time, we came to appreciate our differences.

Appreciate Your Differences
(Jon)

So often the things we are attracted to in the other person initially are the very things that bother us when we are in a relationship with them. When I met Kathryn, I loved her spontaneity and ability to embrace the moment. She could command a room. She was such an outgoing, fun-loving, happy, smiling light. I wanted to be more like that, so I was drawn to her.

But when we were married and had children, I wanted her to be more structured, focused, and detail oriented. I wanted her to be more like me. But that's not who she was. That's not who I married. We often marry someone and then we want to change the person into our image or expectation of what they should be.

If Kathryn wasn't so strong, I probably would have broken her and lost what made her special in the process. She would have lost herself and been miserable and we would surely have divorced. But she fought back. She didn't take my crap. She knew who she was. I had a choice. I could leave and find someone more like me, or I could appreciate our differences.

I would often think, "Do I want someone who cooks in the kitchen all day or do I want someone who loves me and who I love?" "Do I want someone who gets the kids to bed at the same time every night or someone who will have a spontaneous dance party with the kids in the kitchen at the drop of a hat?" Each time I knew the answer.

It took a while but over time I came to appreciate her and what made her different from me. I learned to expect less and appreciate more. The more I did that, I saw all the joy she brought to our family. I realized how much I needed someone like her in my life. Without her I would have been one boring, negative, workaholic, stressed-out man. With her I was becoming a better version of myself. At the time I wanted her to be more like me. Now I'm thankful she stood strong. I appreciated what made her different and now see that they were indeed her strengths, not her weaknesses. And my kids always say what a great and fun mom she was to them growing up.

Shared Vision and Purpose
(Kathryn)

Jon and I were so different. Reading what he wrote brings back the memories of so many of the fights we had. We had such different personalities and expectations that we had to work through. Thank goodness there is one thing that came very easy to us and I believe it's essential for a strong relationship.

We were different but we both wanted the same things out of life. We had the same priorities. We shared the same vision. Through all the challenges and fights, we wanted to be in a great marriage. Family was very important to us. Our kids were our focus. We liked nice things but weren't materialistic. Happiness was more important than money. A family vacation to spend quality time together was more important than a new car. We knew what we were working toward and why we were doing it. We were a team who wanted to raise great kids and we worked together to make that happen.

Your purpose has to be greater than your challenges and your vision has to be greater than your circumstances. If you have a shared vision of the future you are trying to create together and know why you are doing it, you will overcome the obstacles along the way.

If you don't know what your vision and purpose are, I encourage you to think about this with your mate and create a shared vision and purpose. Decide what you want to create together and keep communicating with each other as you work to create it.

Common Bonds
(Kathryn)

In a relationship you are going to have a lot of differences: personality differences, different opinions and expectations, different hobbies. Jon loves watching football; I love yoga. You might have different upbringings and beliefs about food, exercise, politics, faith, and a million other things.

While it's important to appreciate your differences and have a shared vision and purpose, you also want to focus on finding common ground. Identify the things you like to do together. What do you have in common? What are the common bonds that bring you together? Invest your time and energy in those things.

Despite Jon and I being so different, we had a lot of common bonds. We loved watching movies. We loved the same restaurants. We were into organic foods and healthy eating. We both made exercise and working out a priority. We liked a lot of the same people and things. We had the same beliefs about faith and politics. We had similar approaches to parenting and discipline. We actually liked hanging out together when we were by ourselves and we laughed a lot together. Jon knew how to make me laugh and we had a lot of inside jokes that only come from having shared experiences.

I know what I'm about to say is going to make Jon blush, but our sex life was a common bond as well. While sex wasn't something that brought us together, as our marriage evolved it was something that bonded us together. Over time we grew more physically attracted to each other and I think that's because I felt like he was *for* me, not against me. The more he lifted me up with support and encouragement, the sexier he became. Who can be attracted to someone who's always beating you down? So no matter what was going on in our lives, we made time for physical connection. Even when

55

I = Invest

he came home late from traveling and I was tired and stressed with the kids and not interested, I still made the effort and it really helped us connect.

That's why I always encourage women to have sex with their partner! It's biologically designed to create a bond. It shouldn't be your only common bond but it can be an integral part of what bonds you together.

There's No Plan B
(Jon)

When you are making big life decisions, communicating and finding common ground is more important than ever. When Kathryn and I talked about moving to Ponte Vedra from Atlanta, I remember Kathryn saying, "We are young; what do we have to lose? Let's go for it." When we decided to take a second mortgage on our home and open our first Moe's Southwest Grill, Kathryn said, "If it fails we will have to start over, but let's go for it." I agreed and we took the leap. When I started writing and speaking, Kathryn was fully supportive of that too. I eventually opened four Moe's Southwest Grills and had managers operating each store and a managing director who oversaw them. I handled the marketing while also growing my speaking business.

A lot of speaking opportunities came from word of mouth and from readers of my weekly newsletter that I started in 2002. Over the next few years I would hustle and market, market and hustle, and speak anywhere to any group that would invite me. I remember driving down to West Palm to speak at an event that had been canceled (no one told me), only to turn around and drive back home the same day. I spoke at local chamber of commerce meetings, friends' sales meetings, women's groups, car dealerships, high school sports teams, insurance and real estate offices, and local schools.

A big break happened when I got on the *Today Show* to do a series called "Get Energized Today." I had been visiting my parents when I ran into a friend from high school, Mark Rathjen. I randomly asked him if he knew anyone who worked for *Good Morning America* or the *Today Show*. He actually did, someone he went to college with. He sent her my marketing materials and a book I had written, and she booked me for a four-week series.

I thought my career was going to take off. I was going to be the next Wayne Dyer. My book would sell millions of copies.

The series went great and I was told to get ready because my life was about to change. It did change a little in that I received requests to speak in different cities at different events that helped get my name out, but besides that not much else happened. Book sales took off for a few weeks but then slowed down. It wasn't like I became a household name. But I was making progress, and was happy about that.

On the other hand, the restaurants were draining me. It was one problem after another. One day the power went out. Another day someone was caught stealing. Another day people didn't show up for work. Then another franchisee came into town; since I hadn't bought the exclusive franchise rights in our city, he opened up a few Moe's not too far from me. They started to cannibalize my business.

I was flying to Portland, Oregon, to speak at an insurance event, feeling grateful in one moment that someone was paying to fly me to speak and do what I love and in the next moment thinking about the restaurants and feeling frustrated and tired. I picked up a business magazine and started reading an article called "How to Know When to Sell Your Business." Hmmm, I thought. Maybe it's time to sell.

I gave my speech and loved it. I felt energized. Then on my way home I was reading a different magazine, and saw an article called "How to Value Your Business When Selling." It was a sign. I knew it was time to sell the restaurants. I felt like God was giving me the message loud and clear.

I walked in the door and told Kathryn about the signs and that it was time to sell the restaurants and that I was meant to focus completely on writing and speaking. The time was right. Kathryn reminded me that the restaurants were providing for our family and that I wasn't making a lot as a writer and speaker. I spoke a few times a month and made five thousand some months and nothing other months.

I said, "We will live off of the money from the sale of the restaurants until I can make it as a speaker."

She asked, "What happens if you don't make it?"

I told her, "There are no other options. There's no plan B."

All In
(Kathryn)

I was honestly scared when Jon said he wanted to sell the restaurants. We were always struggling with money and were finally stable and in a good place. I was finally a bit comfortable. I didn't want to lose what we had. I also didn't want to go back to a time when we fought about money again.

It wasn't that I didn't believe in him. I just didn't see proof that speaking and writing was a viable profession. I felt better when he said we could live off of the money from the sale for a while, but I kept wondering what we would do if he didn't make it. What if we burned through all our money while he pursued his dream? What would we do if he couldn't make a living doing it?

It was a big risk. But Jon was adamant about it. This was his passion and he wanted to go for it. So after the initial shock I agreed to sell and we went all in. Jon asked the other franchisee in town if he wanted to buy his restaurants, and thankfully he did.

They went through the due diligence process. We were on vacation at one of our favorite places, Woodloch Pines in the Pocono Mountains, when Jon got a call that they wanted to delay the sale a few months. This did not sit well with me. We were charging ahead in a different direction. Jon had already told his managing director about the sale and they had already taken a lot of steps that would make it hard to delay; it would be very damaging to the business to delay the sale. I told Jon he needed to call them back and say that we needed to move forward with the sale on the date we scheduled and that delaying wasn't an option. The buyer agreed and a few weeks later we officially sold the restaurants.

It was 2005 and Jon was free from the burden of the restaurants. He was now a full-time writer and speaker, but it wasn't too long before the excitement wore off and he became fearful and stressed again.

Choosing Faith

(Jon)

It had been six months since we sold the restaurants and speaking and book sales had dried up. My career didn't take off like the experts said it would. In fact, it seemed like my career was regressing. Everything just stopped. I still had enough money to carry us for another year, but watching a lot of it leave our account after six months was scary. I was working on feeding myself with positivity, but nothing could take away the anxiety and fear I felt.

My friend Daniel Decker, who was working with me to grow my speaking business, gave me a few CDs with sermons from pastors. One sermon explained that Jesus was a Jewish rabbi and there was a reason why the young men who became his disciples would follow him. The other sermon from Erwin McManus was called "Why I Follow Jesus." It was heartfelt and powerful and really spoke to me.

Growing up in a family with a Jewish mom and a Catholic dad who never went to church or temple, I never thought about Jesus. I was told he was a teacher and a prophet and never explored anything beyond that. Now I was exposed to a completely different story and perspective and it resonated with me. I prayed a simple prayer. "God, if there is something to this Jesus, if he is who he said he is, show me the signs. I'm open."

Very soon after that I started to see signs everywhere. I literally saw signs on the road. It happened so often it made me laugh. But one time really stood out. I was driving to Orlando to give a talk and while looking to the left I heard the word "look" and when I turned my head to the right, I saw it: a large billboard with bold

I = Invest

letters: "Jesus is the answer." What is he the answer to? I wondered.

Then while meditating—which I tried to do daily—I started seeing a glowing cross. It may sound crazy, but it's true. I grew up on Long Island, New York. My mom was Jewish. My dad never talked about Jesus, ever. I never thought about Jesus and now I was seeing a glowing cross.

A week later I visited a Buddhist energy healer named Don Van Vleet. I was having stomach and colon issues and his treatments were helping. I told Don about seeing these Jesus signs and asked him what he thought of it. He said, "Oh, Jesus is God's system for taking our soul pain."

"What!?"

"Christians call it sin. I call it soul pain. If you have this soul pain, which is heavy vibrational energy, you can't connect with a perfect harmonious energetic God. Jesus takes it so you can connect with God."

I asked Don if I could take someone's soul pain from them.

He asked, "Can you handle your own?"

I knew the answer. No, I couldn't. I was stressed, anxious, and fearful and no matter what I tried I couldn't get rid of the nervous pit in my stomach. The anxiety wouldn't go away. I tried every new age and spiritual technique out there. Nothing would take my soul pain.

Then Don said, "Jesus is like spiritual cheating. You see, I want to see if I can obtain enlightenment like Buddha. I want to do the work and do it on my own. With Jesus all you do is believe and receive."

Even before I wrote *The Energy Bus,* I was an energy guy. I saw everything as energy, which Einstein explained clearly in his formula $E=mc^2$. Don's explanation made so much sense to me. I believed that God would want to take my soul pain and burden so I could connect with God. I believed God would make it simple and easy. Man clutters. God simplifies.

I walked out of there believing that God would want to save me and I said I was going to give this Jesus a shot. I didn't know everything. I didn't have all the answers. I just chose to have faith and that began a journey that would change everything.

When You Change, the Relationship Changes
(Kathryn)

When Jon told me about his conversation with Don, I was intrigued. This is new. Let's see where this goes.

I had grown up in an Irish Catholic family and beyond Christmas and Easter and going to church with friends after sleepovers as a kid, I wasn't a regular churchgoer. But I did have a Catholic great aunt who lived 100% by her faith and she was such a positive influence on my family growing up. So I saw how having a strong faith made you a good human being.

It was surprising to me that my husband was now talking about Jesus. For years Jon wanted me to change to be more like him and I wanted him to change, not to be like me, but to be the kind, loving man he was when we were dating. It wasn't immediate but I noticed subtle changes. He had more patience. He was reading books and listening to more sermons. He had more compassion for me and for the kids.

I realized that you can want someone to change but you can't make them change. You can give them an ultimatum but they have to be the one who changes.

He had made progress since I gave him the ultimatum. But this was different. His heart was changing. His essence was different. This was when our relationship really started to improve. When Jon changed, our marriage changed for the better.

His transformation would also change me. I'll go into that later but for now I just want to say that if you want to improve your relationship, start by improving yourself. When you change for the better, you also change the relationship for the better.

Hopping on the Energy Bus
(Jon)

There was a reason why the *Today Show* appearances didn't change my life and my career didn't take off. If it had, I would not have become the man, husband, father, and author I was meant to be. I felt like God used this idle time in my life to mold and shape me. I was always focused on me and now I was thinking more about ways I could serve, help, and encourage others. With the restaurants sold and only a few speaking engagements on the calendar, I had a lot of time to think, walk, pray, and write. Time slowed down and the world became quieter and still. It felt like I was in a desert experiencing a drought but my roots were growing deeper. My heart was opening and my soul was healing.

One day I was taking a walk and praying about the future. I wondered what I would do if writing and speaking didn't work out. Would I get a job or start another business? Then I thought maybe I should write a fable. I loved reading fables, and my hero Ken Blanchard wrote fables, so maybe I should do that. I wanted to encourage others the way those books encouraged me. What fable would I write?

Then boom! It came to me. The Energy Bus! I would write a fable about a bus driver who changes the life of a passenger and teaches him the ten rules for the ride of his life. It would be about fueling his life, work, and team with positive energy. I had a vision for the book and went immediately to my home office and started writing.

The main character, George, was miserable, negative, and based on me. Joy, the bus driver, was kind, positive, loving, and strong. She and a cast of characters would guide George from being negative to positive. I never wrote a fable before but I wrote the book in three and a half weeks of divine inspiration. I was baptized during this time on Palm Sunday and that experience, combined with writing that book, was the most spiritual time of my life.

I had a vision for the story but I didn't have all ten rules. Each day I would get up early and write, then walk and pray, get new ideas, and come back and write some more. It was as if the story was gradually being told to me each day and all I had to do was show up with an open heart and mind and write. It was magical, mystical, and spiritual.

I finished the book and my agent shared it with publishers. Because sales of my previous book weren't good despite being on the *Today Show,* I received a bunch of rejections. Then I received some more. As always, Kathryn was very supportive during this time. She would say, "They aren't the ones who are meant to publish it. The right one will come along."

Although I appreciated what she said, I often doubted that it would happen. I felt like I had written something special but perhaps I was delusional. Maybe it wasn't as good as I thought it was.

It was a really tough time because after each rejection I felt like my dream was dying. And at the same time my mom was dying of cancer. We didn't know how bad it really was since she and my dad didn't tell us much, but the cancer was spreading quickly.

While this was happening, the rejections kept coming in. After about 30 or more rejections, my agent said that I should probably give up trying to get published and self-publish instead. At that time, self-publishing wasn't as easy or accepted as it is now, so that wasn't an option. I couldn't give up. I had a vision to encourage and inspire as many people as possible, one person at a time, with this book. So I kept hoping, dreaming, and praying that it would happen.

Finally, I got a call that John Wiley & Sons wanted to publish the book. They couldn't give me a big advance but they could release the book in six months and it would come out in January 2007. I didn't care about the advance. I would have let them publish it with no advance. I agreed and waited eagerly for the book to be published. My mom passed away during this time, but I'll always remember her reading the manuscript and enjoying the book. I dedicated the book to her and hoped that I could leave a legacy of love in my children like she left in me.

When the book was published it became a huge hit—in South Korea, not the US. The book was a top-five best seller in South Korea but not one bookstore in the United States would carry the book. I had prayed for it to be a best seller but I learned that you have to be specific with your prayers.

I had to do something to get the book out there. I talked to Kathryn about going on a tour to multiple cities to promote the book. As always, she supported me and told me to go share my message. We decided I would go on a 28-city tour to promote the book and she and the kids would join me in LA and visit a bunch of cities with me as we made our way back to the East Coast.

After visiting a number of cities on my way to the West Coast I finally made it to LA, where Kathryn and the kids flew out to meet me. Jade was nine and Cole was seven. After some fun family time and a few events on the West Coast, our idyllic vision of driving from city to city back to Florida as a family lost its appeal as the kids fought constantly in the back seat of our Ford Aviator, which was wrapped with yellow Energy Bus signage. Kathryn and the kids had enough and decided to fly back home to Florida.

I pressed on, visiting the remaining cities, which only had about 10 to 50 people at each event. While I was driving, Daniel Decker was calling radio shows and morning TV shows to have me on the air, and then we would promote where I would be speaking and signing books.

My college intern Jim Van Allan flew to meet me in the Midwest, which was a good thing because I got sick in Kansas and Nebraska. I slept while he drove. We would show up to an event: I would power through the speaking and get back in the car and fall asleep again. Our biggest audience was 50 people in Austin and 100 people in Des Moines.

It wasn't a successful tour but it was a great test to really live my mission and vision of encouraging as many people as possible, one person at a time. In some cities where there were only five or ten people, I could literally encourage one person at a time. This was when I really learned to make a difference, where I was with the people right in front of me.

It wasn't glamorous. There were no big stages. It entailed driving thousands of miles, staying in cheap hotels, throwing up in Kansas, battling a fever in Nebraska, and still encouraging and serving the people who came to see me. It was honoring the commitment I made when I lost my job during the dot.com crash. I had asked God to provide for me and my family and had said I would do His work. I felt like this was the work He wanted me to do and I was committed to it.

I arrived home three weeks after last seeing my family. I was exhausted, humbled, and heartbroken from missing my family. I walked in the door, collapsed on the floor, and just wept as Kathryn hugged me. I was unsure about my future but I knew more than ever that wherever Kathryn and my kids were, that was where my home was. It wasn't a house or a place. It was the people I loved and who loved me. Kathryn hugged me even tighter.

You know you're with the right person when they give you strength. She gave me strength. She supported me through all of it. I would not have been able to do this work and go on this journey without her.

Support Instead of Limit
(Kathryn)

Jon had changed a lot. I had witnessed his transformation. I knew his mission and purpose was pure. He had gone from being narcissistic and self-serving to someone who wanted to serve others. He was driven for the right reasons and I was driven to support him.

Of course, I wasn't crazy about him being gone for so long, but I also didn't want to get in the way of his mission. Being the daughter of a father in the Navy, I saw my dad leave often to carry out the mission he was assigned and return later to his family. While Jon and I know a book tour and being gone for speaking engagements doesn't remotely compare to the mission and the long stretches someone in the military embarks on, we both had a missional approach to his work and I saw it as my job to encourage and support him in that.

I know women who are worried about their husbands being successful, so they hold them back. Their insecurity causes them to say, "Stay with me," instead of, "Go do the work you are meant to do." The wife doesn't support the husband and he doesn't feel free to do what he needs to do to be successful for himself and his family. In the long run, this doesn't help either person.

I'm not saying that if your partner has a crazy idea that you don't think will work that you should just say, "Sure, go for it." Just as a plane has a pilot and a copilot and a process of communication and procedure to avoid the human error of one person, you can avoid big mistakes by discussing it together. But what I *am* saying is that you shouldn't let your fear and insecurity keep you from supporting them and they shouldn't let their fears limit you.

One thing Jon did right early on was that he encouraged me to leave the sales job I hated and pursue acting. I did a bunch of commercials, was in a play, did a standup comedy routine, and fulfilled a dream and desire I always had before having my children. He supported me early on and now I was supporting him.

Don't limit each other's potential. Support each other as you become the best version of yourselves and pursue your goals and dreams together.

Encourage Instead of Compete
(Kathryn)

In order to pursue your goals and dreams together you need to encourage each other instead of competing with one another.

One of the challenges I see couples face is that they vie against each other instead of providing support. They don't have a shared vision and mission as I talked about earlier. They are two individuals instead of one team.

I know couples who compete in their dieting. If their spouse loses more weight, they are jealous instead of happy for them. If one is working out and making strides in the gym, the other one doesn't like that. I know some couples who compete about whose job is more important or should take precedence.

It's okay to have individual goals and dreams, but they must serve the vision and purpose you have as a couple. Relationship GRIT doesn't happen if you are competing against each other. It happens when you are for each other and encourage each other. You can't be two separate teams. You have to be one team.

The 4 Cs

(Jon)

I love what Kathryn said and I think it's a great segue to finish this chapter with the 4 Cs. Over the years I've made a lot of mistakes and I've learned a lot from them. As someone who now works with a lot of teams to improve their relationships, I wrote *The Power of a Positive Team* and afterward I heard from people that they utilized the 4 Cs not only at work but in their relationship as well. So I thought it would be helpful to recap them and share them with you.

The fact is that to have a great relationship, you must invest time and energy in your relationship. You must become one team. The 4 Cs are a simple, practical, and powerful way to help you do this.

The First C Is **Communicate**

The foundation of every relationship begins with great communication.

Unfortunately, many relationships suffer from poor communication. A lack of communication leads to voids, and where there is a void in communication, negativity will fill it. We must make time to communicate consistently and constantly in order to fill the void.

As Kathryn shared earlier, you must communicate, communicate, and communicate. In a world filled with busyness, stress, and distractions, it's becoming harder to communicate, and our relationships are suffering as a result. It takes more time, focus, and effort, but when you slow down and communicate you are able to build a stronger bond and relationship.

If you have trouble beginning the process, there's nothing wrong with seeing a counselor together. Sometimes we all need a coach to guide us toward improvement. A counselor can help coach you and your spouse to be better communicators.

The Second C Is **Connect**

Communication begins the process of building trust, but connection is where a bond of trust is created. You don't just want to communicate. You want to communicate to connect.

Connecting is essential because you'll never have commitment without connection. If you want a committed relationship, you must make the time to connect with each other. Some couples connect by having a weekly date night. Other couples eat dinner together and talk about the day. Kathryn and I connected by taking walks together at night. We also did a number of other things that we'll share in the next chapter.

The key is to find time for meaningful conversation. Be vulnerable with each other. Share your struggles and fears. Listen to each other. Support each other. Help each other feel seen and heard. When this happens you develop a bond of trust, along with psychological and emotional safety. Teams that have psychological and emotional safety develop a greater commitment to each other, and the same goes for marriages as well.

The Third C Is **Commit**

When you connect with each other you will become more committed to each other. But commitment also requires you to actively commit.

What does it mean to commit? It means you honor your relationship, something I didn't do early on. I'll share more about that soon. It means you serve each other, which is something I still hadn't done well up to this point in our marriage. Kathryn was always committed but it took me a while to learn what commitment truly meant. I'll share how I finally committed in the next chapter.

Committing also means that at times you sacrifice your own desires for the good of the relationship. That might mean something as big as moving to a new city you don't like for your spouse's job, or something small like going with your wife to an event instead of watching the game you have been excited to see. It also means giving your spouse your time and attention when they want to share something with you or ask you for your help or affection. In fact, research by psychologist John Gottman and Janice Driver shows that partners who frequently make time to honor the request of their spouse are more likely to stay together. It all comes down to making the time and the effort to be there for each other.

The Fourth C Is **Care**

The reason why you will make the time and effort to communicate, connect, and commit is because you care. If you didn't care, you wouldn't invest the energy or make the commitment.

In great relationships, the couple cares more about each other and the relationship, so they give their all to each other. They do whatever it takes to make the relationship better. They don't just go through the motions. Because they care more, they do more, give more, and become more.

Caring really is the difference between a good relationship and a great one. Too often we allow busyness and stress to prevent us from caring about the people we are supposed to care about, including our mate. The key is to find practical and meaningful ways to show you care. Kathryn and I will share a bunch of ideas in the next chapter, which is all about investing together.

Chapter 4

T = Together

*When you have Relationship GRIT, you don't give up
when things are hard. You work together and invest
in your relationship, and through the process you
become stronger together.*

Going Deeper

(Kathryn)

It was February 2010 and at that time Jon and I had a good marriage but it wasn't a great marriage. We had done a lot of things right and had grown together rather than apart, but the circumstances of our life didn't allow a lot of time for connecting at a deeper level. He was often on the road speaking and when he came home we were both engaged with the kids and doing things as a family. It wasn't a bad thing. It's just the way things were at that time. We were happy and it was all we knew. Only later would we know what we were missing. It's like having a piece of cake and enjoying it but you don't realize that it was just *good* until you have a *great* piece of cake.

We were invited by Jon's friends to attend an FCA (Fellowship of Christian Athletes) couple's weekend in Naples, Florida, where there would be speakers and music and free time to play tennis and have fun together. Soon after we arrived, I pulled my back and it hurt even to walk. So all the plans we had to play tennis and exercise and ride bikes together were squashed. It felt like we were being forced to slow down and not do anything but just be together. The first night we listened to speakers and worship music, met some great couples, and spent time in prayer.

Jon had spent a lot of time growing in his faith and I honestly hadn't spent a lot of time on mine. He would read different passages to me and explain certain sermons he had heard. He always shared it in a way that made sense to me and did so in a loving way. But I wasn't seeking information or growing on my own.

That all changed when I heard Anne Graham Lotz speak the second night. She is the daughter of Billy Graham, and as she spoke and shared her message about our need for God and His love for us, I just started to cry. My crying then turned to an uncontrollable weeping and sobbing that I couldn't stop. The faucet had opened and all my fears and burdens and pain just came pouring out of me. It was one of the most powerful moments of my life.

I felt more open and connected to God after that and more connected to Jon. I can't explain why or how this works or happens. I just felt like God was opening my heart and cleansing my soul. After that I had a deeper, more intimate connection with God that paved the way for a deeper, more intimate connection with Jon.

Invest in the Root If You Want the Fruit
(Jon)

When Kathryn started weeping, I heard the words, "You thought you came here for you? You came here for her."

One of the reasons I wanted to go to this FCA event was to connect with the FCA leaders and meet some of the great speakers they had that weekend. I had read their books and loved their messages. I had also just written my book *Training Camp* and some of my friends in FCA who read it said it would be a great message for coaches around the country. So I thought we were there for all these terrific opportunities, but the minute Kathryn began to weep God showed me that we were there for her; for her to grow deeper in her relationship with God and for us to go deeper together. We weren't there for me. We were there for her and for us.

Relationship GRIT doesn't happen by accident. It happens when you invest together. And the key word here is *together*. It can't be one person who makes the investment. Both have to make it.

Before this moment, Kathryn and I had a good relationship. She invested in us more than I invested in us. And I invested in God more than she did. But it became great when I invested more in us and she invested more in God. We both had to invest in the root and what really mattered if we wanted to experience the fruit of a great relationship.

This chapter brings G-R-I-T all together. When you make **G**od the center of your relationship and you **R**esolve to stay together and **I**nvest in your relationship **T**ogether, you not only develop Relationship GRIT, you also create a special relationship filled with more love, joy, laughter, intimacy, and commitment than you ever thought possible. Ironically, I learned all this about relationships after I almost destroyed my marriage.

Clearing Out the Weeds

(Jon)

It was 2010, a few months after our time in Naples, and all the investments I made over the years as a writer and speaker were paying off. A principal I met on my book tour in 2007 invited me to speak at his school and I started to speak to a lot of schools. A business leader I met on the tour brought me in to speak to their company and then a lot of companies started to hire me. Jack Del Rio, the head coach of the Jaguars at the time, invited me to speak to his team and the next thing I know a bunch of sports teams were reaching out and inviting me to speak. My one-person-at-a-time approach grew my platform and impact exponentially. I was reaching more people and touching more lives. My career as a writer and speaker was blossoming and was becoming everything I dreamed it would be.

My marriage to Kathryn was improving as well, and yet I knew something was holding us back. I kept feeling like I needed to tell her about my infidelity early in our marriage. It wasn't out of guilt that I thought I should tell her, or because I thought it would make me feel better. I didn't want to tell her but I kept feeling like I had to because I knew it was holding us back from going to the next level in our relationship.

I didn't know what the next level was or that greater intimacy was possible. I just kept receiving insights that you can't have a great marriage if you are keeping secrets from each other. It was as if there were some weeds crowding out the root that needed to be cleared out.

I told a friend that I felt God nudging me to tell her. He said because it didn't involve sex, I didn't need to tell her. But I knew he was wrong and that God was right and I needed to break the news.

One day while walking on the beach, Kathryn was talking about a few of her friends who were getting divorced and I said, "I need to tell you something." Maybe it wasn't the best time but I just blurted it all out and gave her the whole truth and nothing but the truth.

I didn't think it would bother her since it had happened more than ten years earlier, but boy, was I wrong. She went from zero to 60 faster than I've ever seen, from tears to feelings of betrayal to anger. She didn't want to talk to me and walked away. I thought it might be the end of our relationship.

The Truth Hurts
(Kathryn)

When Jon shared the news, I felt like I got punched in the stomach. Here I was sharing how my friends were getting divorced and telling him about my fears of getting divorced and then he hit me with the news that made me want to divorce him!

I never thought he could do something like that. I knew he was a jerk but I never thought he was an unfaithful jerk. I was angry and hurt and immediately thought my whole life with him had been a lie. His confession brought up all my fears and issues. I wanted to hurt him back. I was going to cheat on him and show him how it felt. I wanted someone else to look at me the way he could look at another woman like that.

He tried to talk to me but I couldn't even look at him. He explained how he was a different person back then. He talked about how it happened in the early years during our difficult times and how he changed. And while I knew he was right, nothing else mattered in that moment. In that moment he was a liar and a cheater. He said he wasn't proud of his past but he knew it was something that prepared him for being on the road alone as a writer and speaker years later. Because he was ashamed of what he did when he was younger, he would never do something like that ever again and he was better and stronger for it.

While that was all well and good, I just couldn't get over the fact that he would do that to me. My heart was broken. My ego was bruised. My picture of him as a great man was shattered. I was going to join my friends in the divorced category.

A Special Prayer
(Jon)

A few days later I had to travel to deliver a speech at an event. It was so challenging to give a talk about positivity and overcoming challenges when I was going through one of the hardest challenges in my own life. But the rawness of what I was going through made the talk even more powerful.

As I sat on the plane coming home, I felt exhausted and depressed. It seemed so strange to be going through this. The man who was unfaithful back then had radically changed into a different person. The New Testament says that when you give your life to Jesus you become a new creation in Christ. The old you is gone and a new you emerges.

To those who are not of the Christian faith, it may sound strange and may be hard to fathom this, but those who have experienced as I have—and I've met many who experienced the same thing—know that you do become a different person. It's not something you make up in your mind to feel good about yourself or to feel better about what you have done in the past. It's not a get-out-of-jail-free card. It's a spiritual transformation that is hard to explain logically. You are transformed from the inside out. In fact, my friends who knew me when I was younger can attest to how different I am now.

I literally felt like the old me wasn't me. This was me and I was now paying for something that young, stupid guy did. I'm not saying this to abdicate my responsibility or to make an excuse for my actions. No matter how much you change, there are consequences for your past actions and I had to own mine. I just knew the guy who did that back then wasn't who I was now. I always believe people can change for the better because I know I have.

So as I sat on the plane in an aisle seat, I engaged in a meaningful conversation with the guy in the aisle seat across from me. I eventually told him what happened with me and Kathryn. He had no idea who I was but he was very wise and helpful. He then told me that he and his wife say a prayer before bed each night together and it has made a big difference in their marriage. What a great idea—I knew immediately that we needed to do this. He told me his prayer but said Kathryn and I should come up with our own.

The next morning Kathryn still wouldn't talk to me, and I prayed to God to give me a prayer that Kathryn and I should say together. Boom. It came to me in that moment and I wrote it down.

God, we invite you into our marriage. To love us, unite us, heal us, strengthen us, and protect us so we may grow strong together and serve you together.

That night I said the prayer while Kathryn and I were lying in bed together. She still wouldn't talk to me or acknowledge me but I said it knowing it was meant for us. I did it the next night too. And the next night after that. I kept doing it whether she was listening or not.

Forgiveness

(Kathryn)

Jon kept apologizing. He owned his actions. I wouldn't talk to him so he left love notes for me at the coffee machine where I went first thing in the morning. He put them by my sink at night. He left one in my car by the steering wheel.

Then he started saying this prayer at night before bed. He would try to hold my hand but I would pull it away. I was so angry that at first I covered my ears. But he kept saying it and one night I actually heard it and remembered the words. Then a few nights later I actually said it in my head. But I refused to say it aloud. Then one night I reached for his hand and actually said it out loud with him. I think that was the moment I chose to forgive him.

I was hurt but I did love him. I was angry at him but decided I didn't want to divorce him. He was a different person. We had grown so much together. I didn't want to hold on to this bitterness.

To heal, I knew I needed to forgive. It wasn't easy. I grew up with two brothers. I'm a fighter. When you hurt me, I fight back. But you can't fight someone who keeps apologizing and is truly sorry for what they did.

So instead of punching him, I forgave him, and it really was the best thing ever to happen to us. We were at one level in our marriage but after getting over the hurt and talking and healing the wounds, we went to a whole new level of intimacy and love. The prayer worked. God healed us, united us, and strengthened us.

What You Uncover, God Will Cover
(Jon)

I learned so much during this time, but one of the biggest lessons was that if you cover up something it will eventually be uncovered. We see this happen all the time with scandals in the news. Eventually the truth comes out for the world to see. You can only hide it for so long. But if you uncover it yourself and bring it out into the open, God will cover it with His grace. It will become an opportunity to heal and grow stronger together.

In our case there were no longer any secrets between us. The secret was uncovered and God covered it with grace and we became stronger because of it.

A Covenant
(Kathryn)

A few weeks after Jon broke the bad news to me, we were taking a walk together when he told me he had to tell me something. I thought, "Here we go again." But Jon said this was something positive. He was reading about a person having a covenant with God when

God gave Jon an insight that *we* needed to enter into a covenant with God together. He said marriage vows are between us but a covenant is with us and God.

And so on that walk we entered into a covenant where we would be faithful to each other and God for the rest of our lives. This was easy for me because I had always been faithful. And Jon said it was easy for him because he had been faithful for years.

But this wasn't about it being easy. The covenant was more than that. It was about making God the center of our marriage. It was about inviting God into our marriage. It was about our marriage being a sacred union.

At the time I didn't realize how much of an impact it would have on us and our relationship. The covenant and nightly prayer bonded us together and to God. We became a triple-braided cord that could not be broken.

I know that this may sound strange to some who don't have a spiritual or religious foundation, but the covenant and prayer were the two most powerful things we have ever done and we grew together in so many ways after that.

It may also sound strange when you hear that God gave Jon this insight or this prayer just came to him, or he had a knowing he was supposed to do this and that. But it's very real. His books take about three weeks to write. The ideas just come to him. He walks, prays, and listens and the books just flow. He then shares these ideas with others and they benefit millions. He knows he's not special. He's just open and receptive. He knows that his purpose is to make a difference in people's lives.

We wrote this book for the same purpose. We believe a lot of these ideas can help you and your relationship. We also believe if you are open and invite God into your relationship, you will see a transformative impact as we did.

The 5 Ds

(Jon)

Looking back, I see the power and importance of becoming a triple-braided-cord marriage. I see how we bonded together and were able to stay united and connected through our internal and external challenges. The truth is there are constant negative forces that will sabotage your relationship if you aren't bonded together. You need to know this and understand how these negative forces work. You have to find ways to stay strong together so you can overcome them. I've discovered there are 5 Ds that will destroy your relationship if you let them.

The First D Is **Distort**

Negative thoughts are lies that fill your mind and they aren't coming from you. How do I know? You would never actively choose to have a negative thought. They just pop in and distort the truth. They tell you that you aren't good enough for your mate. They tell you that this won't last. They tell you that if your partner really knew you, they wouldn't love you anymore. They tell you that your future is hopeless, or that the grass is greener somewhere else in another relationship with that person who gives you attention while your spouse is busy working or with the kids. They tell you that this is as good as it gets.

The Second D Is **Discourage**

These lies then discourage you. They make you feel *less than* and unworthy. They make you feel like things won't improve and your future is hopeless. They make you want to give up. I've found that we don't give up because it's hard. We give up because we get discouraged. The distortions (lies) discourage us and we feel defeated and stop fighting for the relationship and ultimately we give up.

The Third D Is **Doubt**

The lies and discouragement lead to doubt where we no longer trust our mate, ourselves, or God. We doubt if we are supposed to be together. We doubt that we will be happy with this person. We doubt that our future will be great together. We doubt if we made the right decision to be together.

The Fourth D Is **Distract**

When you are discouraged and doubtful, you become more easily distracted. You look at what seems appealing and move toward it and make bad choices. Or maybe you don't do anything bad. Maybe you just become distracted by something that keeps you from what matters most, like your relationship. It's true that "If the devil won't make you bad, he'll make you busy." He'll get you focused on all the things that don't matter instead of what does matter. This can lead to a bad outcome as well.

The Fifth D Is **Divide**

When truth is distorted and you believe the lies and become discouraged, doubtful, and distracted, this leads to division. You become separated from each other mentally, emotionally, and spiritually. You feel disconnected and divided from your mate and God. This division then often leads to the sixth D, which is divorce. In my work with teams it leads to defeat. A divided team cannot stand. The negative forces in this world divide us from one another and eventually destroy our relationships. The good news is that once you understand how the game is played, you can win. When you see the 5 Ds come your way, you can counter them.

Instead of listening to the distortions (lies), you can see them for what they are and speak truth to them. You can encourage yourself and your mate when you feel discouraged. You can talk about your vision and hopes and dreams together and keep them alive in your hearts and minds. You can trust when you feel doubt. You can trust God with your relationship and trust each other.

This is where the covenant was so powerful for Kathryn and me. When you find yourself being distracted, you can focus on what matters most—your relationship. And instead of letting the Ds divide, utilize the 4 Cs we shared earlier to unite. Communicate honestly and transparently so that truth is always present and lies can't breed and grow. Connect with each other and love each other. Commit to each other. Show you care about each other.

You might be asking how to do this. Well, that's what Kathryn and I want to share with you now. In addition to the prayer and covenant, here are some of our best practices.

Compliment Each Other
(Kathryn)

I complimented Jon a lot and often called him handsome, stud, and my man. I built him up. I let him know I thought he was the greatest man on the planet. I called him smart, hard working, caring, and a great husband and father. I felt I was speaking greatness into him. (This is also a great thing to do if you have children.)

Jon isn't very handy at all. He will admit that. It's not his strength. I didn't focus on his weakness. I didn't make him feel bad about it. I was handy and fixed things

93

T = Together

and didn't give him a hard time for it. I could have, but what good would that have done?

I see too many couples beat each other down. They talk negatively to each other in person and talk about each other in a negative way to their friends. You would think they were enemies, not partners.

Don't get me wrong; I would go off on Jon at times when we were fighting, and there were times I talked to my friends about some of the things that bothered me about him. But this wasn't the norm. I wasn't always bad-mouthing him. Most of the time I was focusing on his good attributes and complimenting him and building him up.

If he lost weight, I told him. If I saw him working with our daughter on her lacrosse stick skills in the backyard, I told him how great it was that he was doing that. And I even complimented him when I didn't want to. There were times he would walk into the kitchen before heading to the airport in his suit looking all handsome and I would have a spark of jealousy (of course it would be when I wasn't feeling great about myself), but instead of not saying anything or even saying something mean, I would tell him how handsome he was and he would beam from ear to ear. It made him feel great before heading out on the road and it created a healthy dynamic.

Who do you want to be with? The person who always tears you down and makes you feel like a failure, or the one who makes you feel great about yourself?

Focus on What They Are Doing Right

(Jon)

Kathryn really did build me up. She made me feel like I could conquer the world. She often believed in me more than I believed in myself. She spoke life into me.

In *The One Minute Manager*, Ken Blanchard talks about the fact that the more you praise someone for what they are doing right, the more often they will do things right. It works in business. It works in sports. It works with kids, and it works for spouses too. So often we focus on what the other person is doing wrong. We focus on their weakness, not their strengths. We tell them all the time what they can do better instead of what they are doing well. Of course, there will be times we need to address something that is wrong in order to help the person improve. That's where the difficult conversations come in. But for most relationships, we need more positive interactions, praise, and encouragement.

Early on I tended to focus on the one thing Kathryn did wrong, not all the things she did right. As you saw, it was a recipe for disaster. But over time I learned to compliment her a lot more and focus on what she was doing right. I told her how beautiful she was and how strong she was. I let her know that I could not have done any of this without her. Where in the past her ADD bothered me, I now recognized her genius and creativity. And when Kathryn started sharing advice to women in person and on social media, I told her the truth. She's a better writer than I am.

It's funny—the more you compliment your mate, the more you like them and the more you like yourself. Complimenting and focusing on what your mate is doing right is like a positive boomerang that comes back to you.

Make Her Your Queen
(Jon)

I grew up with a working mom in the 1970s. When I met Kathryn she was in sales, and along the way she helped me in all aspects of our various businesses. She owns some properties on her own that she manages. My daughter is also a very independent, strong-willed woman. So when I say make her your queen, I hope you know I'm not being chauvinistic or old-fashioned. I believe in equal pay. I believe women are amazing leaders. I've spoken to many of their teams and organizations. I know how dynamic they are.

In my talks I say that while I may lead a team at work and teach leadership to millions of people, I'm second in command of my team at home. Actually, when my daughter is home, I'm third in command. So when I say "queen," I'm referring to a woman as a leader with the utmost power and authority.

If you met the Queen of England, you would treat her extra special. I believe the same goes with your mate. As a man, I believe it's our duty to honor, value, and respect her and treat her like the queen she is and give her the respect she deserves.

Even early in our marriage, despite our fighting, challenges, and my negativity, I still tried to treat her like a queen. When we would buy a new car, she drove it and I drove the old one. As soon as I was able, I bought insurance to make sure she would be taken care of if I died. I took every major decision to her before deciding. I dedicated many of my books to her. When we traveled and I was upgraded to first class, I gave her the seat and I sat in coach. I massaged her when her neck was bothering her.

I did a lot of little things I just mentioned to compliment her and praise her, to make her feel like a queen, and I think it's another reason she stayed in the relationship when things were tough. It has helped us have a great relationship over time. If you make her your queen, she will make you her king.

Make Him Your King

(Kathryn)

Over time Jon did make me his queen. As the years went by, he treated me better and better.

Like the chicken or the egg, I'm not sure what comes first, but I do know that him making me his queen and me making him my king was a big key to the growth of our relationship. I found the more I made him my king, the more he felt like a king who wanted to honor this role. As I said, I complimented him, supported him, built him up, and believed in him to make him feel like a king who had the confidence to take on the world.

Sometimes treating him like a king was as simple as food, a clean house, and sex—not necessarily in that order.

I know this may sound like a generalization, but I do think men are simple creatures. Most men only want and need a few things to be happy. If you can make him feel loved, supported, strong, and powerful, it will improve how he feels about himself and how he treats you.

Be Open to Feedback
(Jon)

While it's important to support, encourage, compliment, value, and honor each other, it's also important to be real and make each other better as well. Kathryn wasn't just interested in making me feel like a king. She also wanted to make me a better king, and I felt the same way about her as queen.

Yes, we need a lot more positive conversations in our relationships, but there are times when we need to share the hard truths as well. And it's important during those times that we are open to feedback.

One time Kathryn and I were talking about the kids and the problems they were having and she said that there were things I could do to be a better father. At first I felt defensive and wanted tell her what she could do to be a better mother. But I just said, "Okay, I'm open. Make me better." A few hours later after she went through her list.... I'm just kidding. After about 20 minutes and some really good advice, I said I would work on doing those things and it did make me a better father.

Feedback shared in love and received with humility will help you improve and grow.

Team Meetings

(Kathryn)

One of the best things we ever did, and I wish we did it earlier in our marriage, was to have a weekly team meeting. We started these meetings when the kids were probably 11 and 13 and they usually took place on a Sunday.

I can still hear the groans when we would say, "Family meeting." Everyone had to put down their phone or stop what they were doing. Yes, sometimes that groan was from me. It was usually a rough start but always ended up being productive.

We would sit around the table and talk about our family mission statement and our weekly accomplishments and failures. We would discuss our challenges and offer solutions. We found out so many things our kids were going through and things that were on their minds that we would never have discovered without these meetings. They offered an opportunity for us to connect with one another amidst all the busyness in our lives. Jon would also read something inspirational from a quote book, a devotional, or something he found online. We would finish each meeting in prayer.

Some people meet for dinner like this each night but with our kids playing different sports and practices and Jon's travel schedule, that wasn't always possible. The meeting was a way for us to get centered, focused, connected, and come together to communicate better as a team and take on our challenges together.

This team meeting helped us become a strong family unit. If you don't have children, I encourage you to meet each week as a couple and create time for you to connect and talk about what matters most. We call it a team meeting because you and your partner are a team, and it's helpful to schedule a regular time for you to connect. You can also write this down as a key idea you can implement if you do decide to have a family.

Give Each Other Space

(Jon)

While making time to come together and connect is essential, there's also something to be said for giving each other space.

One key strategy that worked for us later in our marriage was when I came in the door from work or from being on the road, Kathryn waited before she hit me with the bad news, the difficult conversation, or the tough topic that needed to be discussed. I had read research that most arguments occur within the first 20 minutes of walking in the door. So we decided to create a buffer zone and give each other space, and it worked. We created rules of engagement that worked for us and I believe it prevented a lot of fights that would have happened if we didn't take the time to rest, get comfortable, and create a space to mentally and emotionally discuss the hard stuff.

Create Space to Grow

(Kathryn)

Creating space so we didn't fight was very helpful, but even more important was that we created space for each of us to grow. So far we've talked about a lot of ideas for couples to do together, but making time for yourself and your own growth is just as important. It's essential to create your own happiness, grow individually as well as collectively, and find some alone time for yourself.

While Jon was growing as a writer and speaker, I also made time to cultivate my own life with my friends. If you don't have a career, I think it's essential to find a hobby you enjoy. I picked up tennis after work and gained a whole new group of friends through that. When the kids were older, I joined a book club and would attend health and wellness seminars on the weekends with my friends. I volunteered for various fundraisers or events. I developed a whole friend network through my children's sporting events. Because I had created these connections, I didn't resent Jon for being on the road so much and I didn't depend on him to make me happy. This gave Jon the freedom he needed to go do his thing and create an amazing career and life for us. And it made me a whole lot happier as a wife and mother.

I know some of you are so exhausted you feel like you don't have time for one more thing. I get it. But I bet there is something you would like to do that you haven't made time for. When my kids were toddler and preschool age, Jon was either working or traveling, so I didn't have a lot of time or space for growth. But I would put them in the kid zone at the gym just to catch my breath and get a workout in. As the kids got older, I had more space to invest in myself. To be truthful, I actually enjoyed when Jon would leave to go on the road to speak. If he was home for a few weeks straight,

I would finally say, "Don't you have a group to speak to?" I would tell him, "I like when you leave and I love when you come home." I liked my alone time and I also liked missing him to the point that I looked forward to him coming home. With that said, I didn't like when he was gone too long, and there came a time when the kids were older that we did hit a rough patch. Jon will explain what happened next.

Serve

(Jon)

When I read what Kathryn wrote about creating your own space, I realized that we should probably clarify that space is important, but make sure it's not too much space.

There was a time when I was traveling and speaking too much, and it put a strain on our relationship and family. Our marriage was strong. We were doing all the tips we share in this book, but sometimes life happens. Sometimes adversity hits you so fast you aren't ready for it. It was 2013 and our kids were 15 and 13 years old. I was receiving a lot of speaking requests and accepting most of them. Our son was a competitive tennis player and he was traveling all over Florida for tournaments. Kathryn was always with him somewhere in a remote hotel every Friday, Saturday, Sunday, and sometimes Monday. I would be gone most of the week speaking. When he wasn't traveling for tournaments, he had tennis practices all week that she had to drive him across town for, while our daughter had lacrosse practices. During the day Kathryn was making meals because our kids had celiac disease and needed a special diet.

So during this period of our life, the time she had alone while I was away wasn't growth time. It was survival time. I remember her calling after one of my speaking engagements when she told me, "I need your help. You need to stop speaking so much."

"What do you mean?" I said. "This is my mission."

"I know," she replied, "but I need your help. I can't do this alone. We need you at home."

At first I was a little annoyed and didn't understand why she couldn't handle it. It was as if we were going back in time, when I was in law school and she was asking for my help when I was busy and stressed. I asked her why she needed my help.

She explained that our daughter's grades were slipping and our son was struggling with his confidence on the tennis court and they were fighting all the time on the road and it was very stressful. She wasn't resentful. She was just at her breaking point and desperate for help.

I still didn't get why she couldn't handle it. I announced, "Fine, I'll stop doing my job and come help you do yours." I'm not proud that I said that but I was frustrated.

She didn't argue. She just said, "Come help me," in a soft tone.

I said, "Okay, I will."

Unlike the past when I wasn't there for her, I would be there for her now. I was reluctant at first, but I would be there. I stopped accepting most speaking events and instead of doing about 10–15 a month, I only did two or three.

My word for the year was "serve." I thought it meant to serve others in the world with my mission, but now I had to serve at home. I had gone from being on the road all the time doing my thing to suddenly being at home all the time with my wife and kids. I wasn't used to it. I liked coming and going. Now I was just there all the time. It wasn't easy and I was very frustrated. They were all struggling. My daughter wasn't doing her homework. My son was always giving his mom a hard time. Kathryn was a wreck. My team was falling apart and I was surprised at how this could have happened. What was wrong with these people? I admit it: I wanted a different team.

Looking back, it was a huge test for me. Had I really changed? Was I willing to give up all I had achieved for my family? Was I really committed to my marriage and family? My word was *serve* and now I had to live it. I took my daughter to school every day and picked her up. I made sure she did her homework each night and studied for exams. I brought gluten-free food for her lacrosse practices and games. I took my son to some tournaments and began helping him with his confidence.

I made a commitment to myself that whatever Kathryn asked me to do, I had to do. One time when I was in the middle of watching a game on TV, she asked me to go to the grocery store. I didn't want to but I remembered the pact I made, so I just got up from the couch and went. I didn't tell her about this pact. That could have been really dangerous. But my job was to serve and do whatever she and the kids needed.

My big thing was laundry. It felt like I did more laundry in a week than I had previously done in my entire marriage. It seemed like I was always folding laundry or driving the kids somewhere or making them something to eat. When I was on the road in the past, I hadn't had an appreciation for all that Kathryn was doing, but now I did. I saw how, while I was on the road focused on me and my audience, she was focused on the kids and not herself. She was a selfless hero. I realized all she did in a given day and week and how much easier my life on the road was compared to hers at home.

I also saw how it wasn't just the daily fight that takes a toll on you but the grind of doing life week after week, month after month. It was definitely the hardest year of my life. Every bone in my body wanted to focus on me, but I realized I was at my best when I served my family and focused on *we*.

At the end of the year, Kathryn asked me what my word was going to be next year. Then she laughed and said, "Maybe it should be *selfish* because I've never seen you do so much for us at home." I said no, because *serve* was now a part of me.

I realized that I didn't need a different team. I needed to become a better leader. I saw how my commitment to serve them not only made them better, it made me better. I saw how my relationship with my wife and kids improved. I was no longer coaching them from the sidelines. I was in the battle with them and connecting with them at a deeper level.

The following year our son went to a tennis academy, so our home became a lot easier to manage again. I was able to go on the road some more, but I always made sure I wasn't gone too much. I would be forever changed from the experience, and so would our marriage and family.

In the past I talked about positive leadership as a state of mind. From this experience I was able to talk about it from a state of action. I learned what servant leadership was all about and experienced the transformative power of it in my own life.

The funny thing is that after this year with my family I wrote *The Carpenter, The Power of Positive Leadership,* and *The Power of a Positive Team.* Three of my top best-selling books, besides *The Energy Bus,* happened when I made my marriage and family a priority. My career took off after that and my relationship with Kathryn became deeper and stronger than ever.

Make Your Relationship a Priority
(Kathryn)

I had been so strong for so long in our marriage and this was one time I just couldn't fight and overcome. I was beaten down and Jon serving me and the kids like he did during this time was what I needed. He made our relationship and his family a priority over everything else. When he did that it led to so much growth for him and our family. If he had said no and kept speaking a lot during that time, I don't know what we would be like now.

It's a great example that when you invest in the root, you get the fruit. We were so much closer after that. He had a stronger relationship with our kids and he had a much deeper understanding and appreciation for my role. He truly became a king during and after that experience—not a king who gave orders from the castle but one who served those he loved.

A funny thing happened when I was at the chiropractor's office with Cole, who was having back problems from tennis. Jon was at one of the few events he accepted each month. The chiropractor asked where Jon was and I said he was at the World Leaders Conference, speaking with all these famous people. The chiropractor said, "Well, Jon is kinda famous." Cole said, "Not in our house. He does the laundry and takes out the trash." I just laughed out loud.

I think that's the perfect example of what real leadership looks like and what making your relationship a priority looks like. Careers are important. Success is appealing and sexy. We all want to have money for life and the future. But you must remember that the most important investment you can make is in your relationship. Jon and I have both said this in a lot of ways, but now I want to say it directly to you.

Make your relationship your number one priority. It's not always going to be fun. It's often frustrating and difficult. But I know our kids will always remember Jon serving them. They will remember me serving them. They will remember us committing to each other and making our relationship a priority. And when you do, everything else takes care of itself, and I believe you get rewarded for your faithfulness, trust, and commitment.

Find Your Rhythm
(Jon)

I couldn't agree more with what Kathryn said. I'm living proof of what happens when you make your relationship your priority. My greatest successes came when I put my marriage and family first. Kathryn always made me and the kids a priority, and there is no doubt in my mind that we are who we are because of her love and commitment.

Yet I also need to add that making your relationship a priority doesn't mean you don't work hard to build your career, business, or other endeavors. It doesn't mean that there won't be times when you must be devoted to your work and career. It means you don't sacrifice your relationship at the expense of being successful.

There will be times you might have to spend more time at work than you do at home. There will be times you are both working and it's hard to find time for each other. There will be moments when work feels like it's more important than your relationship. The key is to understand that there is a season for everything and there is a rhythm to life. There is a season to plant. A season to work the land. A season to rest. A season to harvest. You will experience seasons in the course of your year and in the course of your life.

I talk to a lot of people who say that when they are at work they feel guilty they are not at home. And when they are at home they are thinking about work. This leads to a double dose of misery. These people are trying to seek work-life balance, but balance is a myth. So don't seek balance. You'll never find it.

Instead, find your rhythm. When you are at work, be engaged at work. When you are at home, be engaged at home. When you are engaged in both places you will feel better about yourself and happier and more productive in all that you do. Find a rhythm that works for you and your relationship.

For example, if you know it's going to be a busy week, make time for a special day. Your rhythm might be five busy days and two days to connect. It might be six and one. Or it might be that you come home every night and have dinner together before heading to a second job. There is no perfect formula. It's about finding a rhythm that works for you and your relationship. If you know it's going to be a busy season at work for a few weeks or months, then plan meaningful time together at the end of that busy time. Be intentional about your relationship and scheduling time for each other.

Kathryn and I were at our best when we would look at the calendar for the year and see when my busy times were and then plan weekends together and family trips accordingly. For us November, December, June, and July were my slower times and that's when we bonded most in our relationship and family. We never tried to achieve balance, but we found a rhythm that worked for us, and the key is to find a rhythm that works for you.

And when things break down as they did for us that one year, then adapt and adjust and find a new rhythm that will ensure you don't ruin your relationship. It happens to all of us. We are human. The 5 Ds will continually try to distract you from what matters most, but when

111

T = Together

you keep regrouping and finding ways to make your relationship a priority and find your rhythm, you'll stay strong together.

Stronger Together
(Kathryn)

After Jon's year of serving, our family meetings became more meaningful and effective. Our fighting decreased significantly. Our love for each other deepened. He became so much more helpful around the house. Our kids blossomed. Although he was becoming a household name, he said his biggest goal was to be a big name in our household. He still did the laundry and drove the kids when needed.

We developed the kind of mutual understanding that only comes from going through life together. Our connection and commitment to each other kept getting stronger every year. My love and passion for him reached depths I didn't know was possible. He became the husband I always wanted. He now drops whatever he's doing for the kids and for me. He always puts us first, even before himself. He's a kind, loving husband and father we all admire. For all the bad stuff in the beginning, the way he is now has made it all worth it.

We've now been married 23 years and together for 25 years. Our son is going to be a junior in college and our daughter just graduated and is now working in Los Angeles. I've been traveling more with Jon and have come to appreciate all he was doing on the road all those years. Late nights, travel delays, canceled flights, big events, encouraging people, serving others, then getting into a car, heading to the airport, and flying to another city to do it again. I'm having a great time with him and I know he is enjoying having a travel companion.

Our relationship is better than ever, and yet I also know we will continue to learn and grow as we move into the next stage of our life. New challenges and tests will emerge, and we will have to continue to invest together if we want to be stronger together.

The funny thing is that when we started writing this book, we fought more than ever. I had all these fears that we wouldn't be able to write it. All our past issues were coming up as we were talking about them again for the book. I felt insecure for the first time in years. It was a painful process to bring all this to the surface.

The 5 Ds were coming at us very hard. I believe they were trying to keep us from writing this book because it's going to make a difference and help a lot of couples stay united and together. I knew it was a test and we just had to stay faithful, keep working, and get better, and that's what we did. Jon would write and then I would come in and edit some of his work and write some more. Then he would sit down and edit some of my work and write some more. We even used the same computer and chair to write this book together.

The process was symbolic of our relationship and this title. When you have Relationship GRIT, you don't give up when things are hard. You work together and invest in your relationship, and you become stronger together through the process.

Jon wasn't initially excited or comfortable about airing our dirty laundry in this book, but he agreed that we needed to do it to help other couples going through challenging times. A big part of healing is using your pain for a purpose, and we hope our past pain and lessons serve a purpose in your life and relationship. We hope this book helps you realize that you can change and your relationship can change for the better. We hope that you will apply the simple G-R-I-T framework to your relationship to grow stronger together. We pray it gives you hope, because sometimes that's what we need most to get from where we are to where we want to be.

If you had told me in the beginning of my marriage with Jon that we would one day write a book like this together, I would have laughed and thought you were crazy. But the fact that we did should give you hope in your relationship. If we can make it, so can you. The fact that we wrote this and you are reading this is proof that miracles are possible and Relationship GRIT can make you stronger together.

There Is No Perfect Formula

(Jon)

In life and in relationships, Kathryn and I know that you are never done learning and growing. And often one of you will have to grow more than the other. In our story, it's clear that I was the one who had to change more. I tell Kathryn all the time she was always great. I had to learn to be a great husband and I'm so thankful she was patient with me. I truly wouldn't be writing books and speaking and making a difference if it wasn't for her. She met me when I was 24 and now at 49 I can say she helped me become the man I am today.

I also know we are not done growing. We will continually be presented with new challenges that cause us to adapt and grow in our relationship. The fact that Kathryn and I wrote this book doesn't mean we have all the answers. While I believe the G-R-I-T (G=God, R=Resolve, I=Invest, T=Together) framework is perfect, there isn't a perfect formula to implement it. We shared our story and lessons and advice to give you principles to implement and ideas and solutions to consider. It's up to you and your mate to find what works for you and take action.

As Kathryn said, if you make your relationship a priority and invest in it together, you should see your relationship improve dramatically. We don't just want you to stay in a relationship for the sake of staying in it so you can say you have grit. We want you to stay

115

in it so you can enjoy the benefits and love that come when you don't give up. Relationship GRIT is not about going through life together with clenched fists. It's about enduring the pain and challenges and moving through them with an open heart, and experiencing more joy and love with a partner as a result.

The Right Words at the Right Time
(Kathryn)

While there is no perfect formula, we also know the right words at the right time can make all the difference. We know that a tip or idea you haven't considered before could be exactly what you need. I received advice from girlfriends and mentors and it helped me get through some tough times and also helped me communicate better with Jon. I was told I needed to "teach him how to treat me." As you read, I worked hard on that, never gave up, and thankfully it led to a great outcome. While he was a slow learner, he eventually got it. ☺

The right advice at the right time can make a difference. In this spirit, in the next section we will each share 11 of our favorite quick tips that you might find helpful. Many appear throughout the book, but we thought it would be helpful to have them in this quick-tip format. We've also included some discussion questions on page 127 for you and your partner to discuss together.

Jon and I wish you the best in your relationship and are rooting for you! God bless you!

11 Quick Tips for a Great Relationship
(Kathryn)

1. **Bring God into your relationship.** Come up with your own couple/family prayer. You will be amazed at how powerful this is.

2. **Communicate your expectations.** This is a big one! As much as I would love for Jon to be a mind reader, he is not. So I try to make my needs and wants clear (and reasonable). Talk about your expectations, listen to your partner's expectations, and talk about how you can both reasonably meet them. This should be an ongoing discussion. For example, if one of you in the relationship is having a difficult time at work that week then that person should talk about it and the other person can offer support. This could mean picking up dinner instead of expecting it to be made.

3. **Have a shared vision.** What do you want to accomplish as a partnership? What do you want to create for your future? What does a successful relationship look like five, ten, or twenty years from now? Have discussions about what's important.

4. **Don't compete!** Encourage and cheer on your mate. Be happy for their personal and professional successes. I know this might sound like a no-brainer but as we said earlier, we have known couples who compete with each other. A lot of times this didn't fare well. Remember: You are on the *same* team.

5. **Give compliments.** Let the best thing they hear about themselves come from *you*. Look for the good. Find the good. Focus on their strengths, not their weaknesses. Compliment them on the things that are important to them.

6. **Don't keep score.** It will never be equal. We tend to focus on what we are giving or doing and then focus on what our partner is not doing or giving. So no one wins. Remember that the goal is to win together.

7. **Appreciate your differences.** You and your partner are two different people. You should not expect the other to act or think exactly like you. Honor what makes them unique. Perhaps you can see that what makes them different is actually a good complement to you.

8. **Teach them how to treat you.** Your partner may not know how to treat you. They may not have had a good role model. Whatever the reason they have for treating you disrespectfully or poorly,

don't allow it. Don't settle for it. Teach them how to treat you well.

9. **Agree to disagree.** Sometimes you won't see eye to eye. You don't have to agree on everything. Your partner may not always think what you think. That's okay. You can still respect each other's opinion and beliefs. Just make sure you're agreeing on the things that matter most.

10. **Do the things that make your partner happy, and be willing to do things your partner doesn't like to do.** You may not always feel like it but do it anyway. And they should do the same for you. There should be some sacrifice on both of your parts. For example: Jon doesn't like to go through the mail, so I do it. Even though I don't like it either.

11. **Take time to be intimate.** We are biologically wired to have intimacy. This releases the hormone oxytocin, which helps you bond. Physical and emotional intimacy are essential ingredients for a healthy and strong relationship.

HAPPY COUPLING!

11 Quick Tips for a Great Relationship

(Jon)

1. **Heal together.** Talk about your pasts. Talk about your issues. Be vulnerable with each other and talk about the wounds you brought into the relationship so you can heal those wounds together. I'm not saying to do this on your first date, but over time you want your relationship to be a safe place where you can nurture and love each other, heal and grow together.

2. **Give each other strength.** Looking back on my life and marriage, there's no way I could have done it without Kathryn. Her love, support, belief, and encouragement gave me strength. She believed in me when no one else did and gave me the confidence to pursue my dreams. Make it your goal to make each other better and give each other the strength to be all you are meant to be.

3. **Be willing.** You have to be willing to change. When Kathryn gave me the ultimatum, I looked at myself and my life and realized she was right. I was willing to change and it led me to do the

work I do now. Because I was willing, I became a positive influence on my wife, children, and others. So be willing to improve and grow. You'll benefit your marriage, your life, and the world.

4. **Make your relationship a priority.** Make it a priority to invest in your relationship rather than take from the relationship. Focus on giving to—instead of taking from—each other and you will build a strong relationship. Countless things will distract you from your relationship if you let them, so remember what matters most. Focus on your relationship. Make it a priority and everything else in your life will work much better.

5. **Communicate, communicate, communicate.** Most relationships initially break down because of poor communication. Where there is a void in communication, negativity will fill it. It's so important to keep the lines of communication open. Kathryn and I have had our share of disagreements over the years but when we learned to truly communicate, it allowed us to grow strong together. Communicate what you need. Communicate what's not working. Communicate about what each of you is doing well. Communicate to connect.

6. **Take one for the team.** Speaking of fighting, it's important to admit when you are wrong. I

certainly have been wrong many times and have admitted it. And I have also admitted I was wrong even when I didn't think I was, because it was more important to me that Kathryn felt loved than for me to be right. I took one for the team so we could be a stronger team. I lost the battle but we won the war. There will be times you have to give and compromise. Do it even if you don't want to, because you care more about your marriage than about being right.

7. **The more I love my wife, the more I love my life.** I'm not talking about the popular phrase "Happy wife, happy life." I'm talking about the fact that the more I focus on loving and serving my wife, the better I feel about myself and my marriage. It's not about what she does for me. It's not about keeping score. It's about me deciding to be selfless and love her, serve her, and be there for her. I've found that when I do this, we both get better. When your mate asks for your time, attention, and help, make sure you honor their request, make time for them, and give them your energy.

8. **Become one team.** As we've mentioned, Kathryn and I have met a lot of couples over the years who seem to compete with one another. Rather than encouraging and supporting their spouse,

they get jealous if the other person is getting fit or enjoying success. Instead of being one team, they function as if they are two separate teams. A great relationship requires you to be one team, supporting and encouraging each other. When you support and advocate for each other, you grow as individuals and also strengthen your team.

9. **Have a shared mission.** Kathryn and I knew that we weren't together just for ourselves. We believed our mission was to raise champions in life who will make a difference in the world. This mission and purpose influenced every decision we made and continues to influence us. A couple with a shared mission doesn't give up when things get hard. They continue to work together to achieve the mission. Kathryn and I know we weren't perfect parents and have made mistakes along the way, but our mission inspired us to give our very best and kept us going through the tough times.

10. **Give each other space—but not too much.** As we shared in the book, it's important to have your own space to grow as individuals, but you don't want to spend too much time away from each other where you grow apart. We found the optimal time apart was three to four days; after seven days it was too long. I can count on one hand the number of times we were away from

each other longer than seven days. I know that not everyone has this luxury and sometimes you will be apart longer, but when possible find the optimum amount of space that works for your relationship.

11. **Keep working at it. Don't quit.** As everyone knows, being in a relationship isn't easy. There's an ebb and flow. Sometimes the relationship is great and sometimes it isn't. Too many give up and quit, thinking the grass is greener. It isn't. When you plant yourself in your relationship and nurture it and invest your time and energy in your spouse, over time you grow into the person and the couple you are meant to be. Relationships are where you learn to give and take and compromise. It's where you work on your individual issues and heal together. It's where a strong family and team begins. Over the years there were times my wife and I went to counseling, took parenting classes, argued, and disliked each other, but we never stopped loving each other and we never stopped working on our marriage. There might have been a few times when it would have been easier to give up, but thank God we didn't. It's all about Relationship GRIT. You stay the course. Keep working at it. Don't give up.

Even though my last tip says don't give up, if you are dealing with abuse, that's a different story, and we encourage you to seek expert advice immediately. Also, we know that in some circumstances sticking it out may not be the right decision. Not every couple is meant to stay together. We have friends who got divorced knowing it wasn't the right fit. Then they found their soul mates and are happier than ever. We realize that Relationship GRIT isn't for every couple. But we believe you shouldn't give up without trying everything possible. ***Our hope is that this book will help many who would have given up but shouldn't give up. Because they read this, they stuck it out and worked it out, and as a result they created a deeper, more connected, loving, intimate, and happier relationship.***

Discussion Questions

1. Do you keep score in your relationship? What are some ways you can support each other instead of keeping score? (Pages 47–48)

2. On a scale of 1 to 10, how well do you communicate with each other? What would make it a 10? (Pages 48–50)

3. Where are the voids in your communication? How can you fill these voids with better communication? (Page 49)

4. Discuss the expectations you have for each other. Are they reasonable or unrealistic? What are some additional things you can do for your mate? What are some compromises you can make? (Pages 50–51)

5. What do you appreciate about each other's differences? (Pages 52–53)

6. In what ways can you expect less and appreciate more? (Pages 52–53)

7. What is your shared vision and purpose? (Pages 53–54)

8. What are some of your common bonds? What do you like to do together? What do you have in common? (Pages 54–56)

9. How can you compliment each other more? (Pages 93–94)

10. What is your mate doing right? Make a list and spend some time sharing it with each other. (Page 95)

11. In what ways can each of you improve your relationship? (Pages 98–99)

12. How can you make your relationship more of a priority? (Pages 108–109)

13. Do you have a good rhythm in your relationship? What rhythm works best for your relationship? How can you improve your rhythm? (Pages 109–112)

14. What is the number one idea each of you has taken from this book?

15. What is the immediate action each of you will take as a result of reading this book?

Our Marriage Prayer

God, we invite you into our marriage. To love us, unite us, heal us, strengthen us, and protect us so we may grow strong together and serve you together.

A card I made for Kathryn for our 15th anniversary.

It was love at first sight.
Your sparking eyes and beautiful face.
A warm embrace.
Goodbye, fate, an awkward date.
Elimination, a surprising call, a visit
and a soul connection.
I knew you were the one for me.
You are my destiny.
God created us to be together and after
fifteen years of marriage,
I love you more than ever!

A card I made for Kathryn for our 20th anniversary.

Today we celebrate twenty years
together and a love that's forever!

I'm thankful God gave me the eyes to see
inside a woman who saw the best in me.

Without you, I wouldn't be who I am.
Our marriage was God's greater plan.

You're my love, my beautiful soulmate.
I'm looking forward to another twenty years
and more to celebrate.

We are just beginning.

We're not done.

The best is yet to come!

Acknowledgments

We would first and foremost like to thank Matt Holt and Shannon Vargo for believing in this book and supporting us in writing it. Thank you to the John Wiley team, including Peter Knox, Sally Baker, and Deborah Schindlar for their great work in getting this book out to the world. We also want to thank Julia Desantis, Caroline Semmler, Dan Britton, Rachel Layne, Jimmy Page, Brendan Suhr, Mike Smith, Dave Gordon, Julie Nee, Darla Neal, Elizabeth Magnano, Heather Diaz, Sharon Porter, Mindy Augustine, Marzena Mignone, Valerie Mason, Daniel Decker, Amy Kelly, Todd Gothberg, and Jim Van Allan for reading and sharing input with us.

About the Authors

Kathryn Gordon is a wife, mother, businesswoman, movie producer, and coauthor of *Relationship GRIT*. A graduate of Old Dominion University, Kathryn became a top producer in sales for several companies before deciding to follow her passion as an actress and model. After the birth of her children, she focused on raising them and helping operate her husband's growing speaking and consulting business. With her children off to college, she has returned for her second act, investing in real estate and movies, mentoring women, supporting several charities, and writing and speaking to audiences about the keys to a great relationship.

Jon Gordon is a husband, father, author, and speaker who has inspired millions of readers around the world. He is the author of 20 books, including eight bestsellers: *The Energy Bus, The Carpenter, Training Camp, You Win in the Locker Room First, The Power of Positive Leadership, The Power of a Positive Team, The Coffee Bean,* and *Stay Positive.* He is passionate about developing positive leaders, organizations, and teams. Connect with Jon at JonGordon.com.

Other Books by Jon Gordon

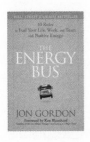

The Energy Bus

A man whose life and career are in shambles learns from a unique bus driver and set of passengers how to overcome adversity. Enjoy an enlightening ride of positive energy that is improving the way leaders lead, employees work, and teams function.

www.TheEnergyBus.com

The No Complaining Rule

Follow a VP of Human Resources who must save herself and her company from ruin and discover proven principles and an actionable plan to win the battle against individual and organizational negativity.

www.NoComplainingRule.com

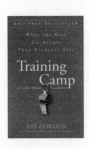

Training Camp

This inspirational story about a small guy with a big heart, and a special coach who guides him on a quest for excellence, reveals the 11 winning habits that separate the best individuals and teams from the rest.

www.TrainingCamp11.com

The Shark and the Goldfish

Delightfully illustrated, this quick read is packed with tips and strategies on how to respond to challenges beyond your control in order to thrive during waves of change.

www.SharkandGoldfish.com

Soup

The newly appointed CEO of a popular soup company is brought in to reinvigorate the brand and bring success back to a company that has fallen on hard times. Through her journey, discover the key ingredients to unite, engage, and inspire teams to create a culture of greatness.

www.Soup11.com

The Seed

Go on a quest for the meaning and passion behind work with Josh, an up-and-comer at his company who is disenchanted with his job. Through Josh's cross-country journey, you'll find surprising new sources of wisdom and inspiration in your own business and life.

www.Seed11.com

One Word

One Word is a simple concept that delivers powerful life change! This quick read will inspire you to simplify your life and work by focusing on just one word for this year. *One Word* creates clarity, power, passion, and life-change. When you find your word, live it, and share it, your life will become more rewarding and exciting than ever.

www.getoneword.com

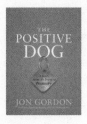

The Positive Dog

We all have two dogs inside of us. One dog is positive, happy, optimistic, and hopeful. The other dog is negative, mad, pessimistic, and fearful. These two dogs often fight inside us, but guess who wins? The one you feed the most. *The Positive Dog* is an inspiring story that not only reveals the strategies and benefits of being positive, but also an essential truth: being positive doesn't just make you better; it makes everyone around you better.

www.feedthepositivedog.com

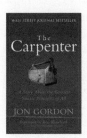

The Carpenter

The Carpenter is Jon Gordon's most inspiring book yet—filled with powerful lessons and success strategies. Michael wakes up in the hospital with a bandage on his head and fear in his heart after collapsing during a morning jog. When Michael finds out the man who saved his life is a carpenter, he visits him and quickly learns that he is more than just a carpenter; he is also a builder of lives, careers, people, and teams. In this journey, you will learn timeless principles to help you stand out, excel, and make an impact on people and the world.

www.carpenter11.com

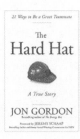

The Hard Hat

A true story about Cornell lacrosse player George Boiardi, *The Hard Hat* is an unforgettable book about a selfless, loyal, joyful, hard-working, competitive, and compassionate leader and teammate, the impact he had on his team and program, and the lessons we can learn from him. This inspirational story will teach you how to build a great team and be the best teammate you can be.

www.hardhat21.com

You Win in the Locker Room First

Based on the extraordinary experiences of NFL Coach Mike Smith and leadership expert Jon Gordon, *You Win in the Locker Room First* offers a rare behind-the-scenes look at one of the most pressure-packed leadership jobs on the planet, and what leaders can learn from these experiences in order to build their own winning teams.

www.wininthelockerroom.com

Life Word

Life Word reveals a simple, powerful tool to help you identify the word that will inspire you to live your best life while leaving your greatest legacy. In the process, you'll discover your *why*, which will help show you how to live with a renewed sense of power, purpose, and passion.

www.getoneword.com/lifeword

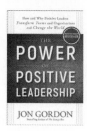

The Power of Positive Leadership

The Power of Positive Leadership is your personal coach for becoming the leader your people deserve. Jon Gordon gathers insights from his best-selling fables to bring you the definitive guide to positive leadership. Difficult times call for leaders who are up to the challenge. Results are the by-product of your culture, teamwork, vision, talent, innovation, execution, and commitment. This book shows you how to bring it all together to become a powerfully positive leader.

www.powerofpositiveleadership.com

The Power of a Positive Team

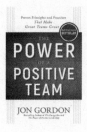

In *The Power of a Positive Team*, Jon Gordon draws upon his unique team-building experience, as well as conversations with some of the greatest teams in history, to provide an essential framework of proven practices to empower teams to work together more effectively and achieve superior results.

www.PowerOfAPositiveTeam.com

The Coffee Bean

From best-selling author Jon Gordon and rising star Damon West comes *The Coffee Bean*: an illustrated fable that teaches readers how to transform their environment, overcome challenges, and create positive change.

www.coffeebeanbook.com

Stay Positive

Fuel yourself and others with positive energy—inspirational quotes and encouraging messages to live by from best-selling author, Jon Gordon. Keep this little book by your side, read from it each day, and feed your mind, body, and soul with the power of positivity.

www.StayPositiveBook.com

The Energy Bus for Kids

The illustrated children's adaptation of the best-selling book *The Energy Bus* tells the story of George, who, with the help of his school bus driver, Joy, learns that if he believes in himself, he'll find the strength to overcome any challenge. His journey teaches kids how to overcome negativity, bullies, and everyday challenges to be their best.

www.EnergyBusKids.com

Thank You and Good Night

Thank You and Good Night is a beautifully illustrated book that shares the heart of gratitude. Jon Gordon takes a little boy and girl on a fun-filled journey from one perfect moonlit night to the next. During their adventurous days and nights, the children explore the people, places, and things they are thankful for.

The Hard Hat for Kids

The Hard Hat for Kids is an illustrated guide to teamwork. Adapted from the best-seller *The Hard Hat*, this uplifting story presents practical insights and life-changing lessons that are immediately applicable to everyday situations, giving kids—and adults—a new outlook on cooperation, friendship, and the selfless nature of true teamwork.

www.HardHatforKids.com

One Word for Kids

If you could choose only one word to help you have your best year ever, what would it be? *Love? Fun? Believe? Brave?* It's probably different for each person. How you find your word is just as important as the word itself. And once you know your word, what do you do with it? In *One Word for Kids*, best-selling author Jon Gordon—along with coauthors Dan Britton and Jimmy Page—asks these questions to children and adults of all ages, teaching an important life lesson in the process.

www.getoneword.com/kids

Other Books by Jon Gordon